LEADERSHIP
WIPEOUT

THE STORY OF AN

EXECUTIVE'S CRASH

AND RESCUE

CHUCK BOLTON

Expert Publishing, Inc.
Andover, Minnesota

ISBN 13: 978-1-931945-44-8
ISBN 10: 1-931945-44-6

Library of Congress Catalog Number: 2005935498

Printed in the United States of America

First Printing: November 2005

10 09 08 07 06   5 4 3 2 1

Expert Publishing, Inc.
14314 Thrush Street NW
Andover, MN 55304-3330
1-877-755-4966
www.expertpublishinginc.com

Jane, John, Sarah, and Alli

Thank you for your love and support and allowing me to do what I love to do!

CONTENTS

ACKNOWLEDGEMENTS

Leadership Wipeout has been fun for me to write and some special people have made it especially enjoyable.

I owe huge thanks to some very special people in my life who have given me years of support, love, and the foundation to do what I do best. Thank you to my wife, Jane, son, John, daughters Sarah and Alli. John and Lindsay, thank you both for bringing Jordan, our beautiful grandson, into the world on September 6, 2005.

Thanks to Mike Berman for his support during our days together at SCIMED and Boston Scientific, his encouragement when I started my executive coaching business and his assistance in helping me simplify the business dilemma that Ben Stevens experiences at CardMedics.

Thanks to Marshall Goldsmith, executive coach extraordinaire, who has taught me the "mini-survey" and "feedforward" concepts and has been so gracious in sharing his knowledge.

Thank you to Bill Tredwell and the team at HayGroup Direct-Boston who have shared their knowledge of emotional intelligence, leadership styles, organizational climate, and have allowed me to adapt some of their materials in our story.

Thanks to my many friends, family, and colleagues who reviewed the manuscript, provided ideas for strengthening the story and wrote testimonials: John Abbott, Karen Armstrong,

Jane Bolton, Steve Bolton, Carolyn Byram, Cindy Carlson, Jim Cornehlsen, Jim Crawford, Bob DeBaun, Bob Elgin, Rich Fellers, Tom Gegax, Marshall Goldsmith, Peter Jacobson, Hank Kucheman, David Lord, Mike Mimnaugh, Diane Owen, Paul Owen, Ralph Polumbo, Rodger Stewart, Bill Tredwell, and Rick Toppin.

Thank you to my writing partner, Brian Bellmont, for your encouragement and making the writing fun. Thanks to marketing and media relations experts Cindy Leines and Kari Logan, website guru Randy Kempenich, designers Tom Heller and Jay Monroe, and editors and publishers Harry and Sharron Stockhausen. Thanks to my assistant, Kerri Murphy, who never complains with my urgent requests for quick turn-arounds and for tolerating too many interrupted evenings and weekends.

Many thanks to the sponsors at my clients who have entrusted me to work with their executives and top teams. Special thanks to: David Bonderud at Baxter Healthcare; Bob Elgin, formerly at St. Jude Medical; Ron Schiferl at Naterra Land; Mark Rauenhorst and Tim Murnane at Opus Group; Jerry Haarmann formerly at Memorial Blood Centers; Bill Lovette and Karen Armstrong at Tyson Foods; Chuck Griffin and Rose Ramon at CarboMedics; Bill Osgood at Cobe Cardiovascular; Rodger Stewart and Carolyn Byram at Sorin Group North America; Giorgio Cottura and Franco Vallana at Sorin Biomedica; Giovanni Caruso at Sorin Group SpA; Eros Roncaia and Judith Thompson at Mitroflow; Rich Effress and Ralph Polumbo, formerly of MedSource Technologies and now at Deephaven Capital Management; Chris Smith at Cochlear Americas; Nancy Chang and Hugo Santos at Tanox; Hank Kucheman, Rick McWhorter, and Tom O'Connell at Boston Scientific; and Lonnie Moulder at MGI Pharma. Thank you to all of my executive coaching clients who have taught me so much and have encouraged me to write this story.

INTRODUCTION

Being an executive today is a highly challenging proposition. The demands leaders face such as the relentless pressure from Wall Street to deliver ever improved financial performance, the crushing workload, the competing priorities, the deadlines, the increasing complexity of a global marketplace, the blurring of personal and work life—well, you get the point!

For quite some time, I've had a burning desire to share with a broader audience, some of the concepts I've learned over the past twenty-five years as an executive in Fortune 500 companies and as an executive coach to senior leaders and their top teams on how to create greater value.

The opportunity and challenge was how best to share this knowledge? There are only so many executives and top leadership teams I can personally coach. So the best avenue to reach this wider audience of leaders, up-and-coming leaders, and those who support them seemed to be in sharing a story—a story featuring protagonist Ben Stevens, with whom leaders will identify. Ben is an executive who struggles at both work and home. He is fallible, very human, and desperately wants to change and be his best.

So last year on a glorious, sunny December day on a ski run in Vail, my idea for a storyline was born. While the characters are fictional, the issues Ben faces and discusses with his ski instructor/coach, Ed Davis, are very real—the same challenges executives struggle with daily.

While I hope you will find this story engaging and informative, what I truly desire is for you to take action in your own life. As you read the story, you'll gain a number of insights that should help you create greater value for yourself, your team and your company. My hope is you will use the teaching points from our story as a framework and inspiration in moving forward to become your best.

Thank you in advance for taking the time to read Leadership Wipeout. I hope you enjoy the story as much as I enjoyed writing it for you.

CHAPTER ONE

From Old Ben to New

My life was careening out of control, and I was headed for a crash.

I was nearly fired from my job and was treading perilously close to alienating my wife and kids. I was a hair's breadth from losing everything that ever meant anything to me.

So it's almost unbelievable that the very thing that saved me, the very thing that helped me start the process of turning everything around, was a spectacular wipeout on the slopes of Vail.

Here's my story.

• • •

You can tell a lot about a guy from what's in his wallet. Mine's a lot like other men's my age—a little worn around the edges and broken in to the point where it fits comfortably in my back pocket.

Right in the middle sits a photo of my wife, Nancy, with her girl-next-door looks and freckled face. She's a nurse at Abbott Northwestern Hospital in Minneapolis and a good one. She's never been one to put up with the way I sometimes get, and I love her for that—and for about a million other reasons. If I find myself sulking and brooding, which I've been known to do on occasion, she quickly and cleanly pulls me out of my funk. If I turn too deeply inward and start to withdraw into a cocoon of intense concentration, she coaxes me back. She knows me better than anyone.

The rest of my wallet is packed with pictures of my kids, Jeff and Amber. I've got photos of them both as plump little babies, a funny one of the two of them on the jungle gym we used to have in our backyard, and a smattering of my favorite school photos.

I'm about due for a new driver's license, which is a good thing because I barely recognize the photo of the man on mine. He's a little pudgier than the leaner guy I am today. He's got a little more hair than I do now. And he's a lot more stressed out. The expression on his face is tight and pained, a combination of lack of sleep, too much coffee, and the weight of the world on his shoulders. Looking at my license now, it seems as if the only thing that's the same about me today is my name. I'm Ben Stevens.

I'm forty-four years old, and Nancy, Amber, Jeff, and I live on Gibson's Point in Deephaven, Minnesota, a western suburb of Minneapolis, on beautiful Lake Minnetonka. We're a happy family, and I'm a contented husband and father with a life and a job I love. But that wasn't always the case.

I'm a particularly fortunate man. In the past year some events and special people in my life caused me to challenge some assumptions and beliefs that no longer worked for me.

I head a division of a large worldwide medical technology company. Our mission is to enhance the quality of life for our customers. You know the old axiom about how the shoemaker's children have the most beaten and battered shoes? That was my reality. At work, I thought I was concentrating on doing everything I could to make our customers' lives better, while my own life was falling apart.

Just over a year ago, I was headed for what you might call a major career derailment. I didn't know it at the time, but it was all my fault. My behaviors and way of being alienated the very people I depended on most at work. And the situation spilled over into my home life, affecting my wife and family, too.

My story is one of transformation, one that perhaps you can relate to. In business terminology, I experienced a "turnaround." I came dangerously close to losing my job and was most definitely isolating myself from the people I cared most about. Over the last year, I've experienced a new beginning, a renaissance of sorts. I've rethought the way I operate with people. I can now connect with and lead others more effectively. I'm not a master by any means, but I feel as though I'm on the right track.

To get here, though, I had to experience some pain. I had a wipeout, both literally (on a mountainside in Colorado) and figuratively (in my business and personal lives). But I'm thankful every day that it happened. That event became a catalyst for my transformation. It was a watershed moment, forcing me to make some important decisions that changed the way I live and work. All the important people in my life–my wife, my kids, my coworkers–refer to my transformation as "The Vail Phenomenon." It's an apt description. I returned from my ski trip with a new outlook on work and family, and a deeper understanding of myself—and the man I wanted to become.

Thank God.

For the past four years, I've been the president of the General Surgery Division of CardMedics, a $4 billion medical technology company headquartered in Minneapolis. I spent nine years in engineering, operations, and a brief stint in marketing before being promoted to my first general management job. I've been a workaholic throughout most of my career. Not long after I accepted the role of president, at about the eighteen-month mark, I was at a real low point. I call this chapter of my life the "Old Ben" period.

I refer to my life at that time as if I was a totally different person, and in a way, I was. Looking back, I'm amazed Old Ben lasted as long as he did. He was always perilously close to self-imploding. But at the time, it seemed like the most natural thing in the world.

Old Ben put in a ton of time at work; he really piled on the hours. His justification for spending so much time at the office, or in the car on the way to or from work, was that he was able to provide a comfortable lifestyle for his family. Achievement became his reason for being. He believed he was smarter than–and could outwork–everyone. He was a "doing" machine.

Old Ben was a competitive, pragmatic, results-oriented guy throughout his career. He was always in control, working long, hard hours and expecting the same of the people he managed. He was a driver and tough on other people. Decisive and opinionated, Old Ben focused on results. He relied on the numbers that had served him so well during the earlier part of his career, back when he was thriving as an engineer. He valued processes more than people. He had a high regard for facts and figures and a low regard for the opinions, feelings, and thoughts of others. He was smart, but he wasn't always right.

Old Ben's operating motto was, "When in stress, press." He was proud of his ability to focus on problems and get them solved by sheer force of his will and effort. He didn't know it, but more than one person he worked with grumbled under their breath that they rarely saw the light with Ben, but they always felt the heat.

Maybe this kind of person sounds familiar. Perhaps Old Ben reminds you of somebody you know. After all, don't these behaviors describe effective executives and leaders? The people we know who get things done? Since I identified my own challenges as a leader, I've found that a lot of people I've run into in the business world share many of these traits. They're extremely effective businesspeople—in the short term. But how can they sustain a growing, thriving enterprise when they're stepping on people along the way?

As I look back on things, I think I must have been sleepwalking through the first twenty years of my career. I had become the person I never wanted to be.

Maybe it's my engineering background at play, but I've always kept a notebook and pen close at hand in case I need to work out a problem or jot down an idea before it gets lost among the thousands of other thoughts jockeying for position in my head. I wrote a lot during the Old Ben period. And the pages of notes I kept from that time in my life make one thing perfectly clear: I was headed for a fall.

What follows is the story of that difficult period, when Old Ben was spiraling out of control. But it also documents his wake-up call, and how he transformed into the man I am today.

CHAPTER TWO

A Terrible Year

To say that work is a bear is an understatement. As I complete my first full year as president of CardMedics' $500 million General Surgery Division, we are failing to meet our annual operating plan commitments. More specifically, we're 9 percent off our sales and 7 percent off our profit plan, with less than two weeks left in the fiscal year. This is simply unacceptable performance and, frankly, I'm embarrassed. To add insult to injury, we just received the third quarter market trend report that shows we're losing market share to our key competitor.

To make matters worse, I was the one who put the budget together, along with my GSLT (General Surgery Leadership Team). As a leadership team, we simply haven't executed. Within the team, there is a lot of finger-pointing, and much of it is directed at me. It's not the most hospitable place for a new divisional president.

I'm hearing all the classic excuses for underperformance. R&D is upset that Operations can't build their new products and release them to Sales on a timely basis. Operations is upset at R&D for designing a product that hasn't been sufficiently specified for manufacturability. Sales is upset at both R&D and Operations because of new product delays—our recently released *CyberLaser* was delayed before it finally hit the marketplace. Sales is also upset with Marketing and Business Development because the sales team feels there have been no new alliances with other companies to bring new products into the fold. There's more than enough blame to go around and, quite frankly, I'm not pleased with my team's business maturity or operating capabilities. They are supposed to be professionals and getting these issues on the table and addressed is part of their job. They're simply not doing what they're paid to do.

Lately, we've been getting more attention from our "friends" at corporate than we would like. When I've attended meetings at the corporate headquarters the past several months, I've felt like a leper. I'm convinced people there are talking about me in hushed voices while avoiding contact and any real, meaningful conversation. Am I being paranoid? Or am I a dead man walking?

The guy I report to, Mike Cole, the Cardiac and General Surgery group president, isn't happy with either this year's performance or with me. Mike is candid and has been quite vocal in his displeasure about our performance shortfall the past several months. Mike and I have never had a close relationship, and that bothers me.

When I received the promotion about eighteen months ago, I knew it was in large part due to the lobbying efforts of my former boss, Phil Watkins, who then worked as group president of Cardiac Rhythm Management. Phil was supportive of me, a great guy I consider a mentor and a friend. Phil was Mike's peer until Phil retired almost a year ago. I subsequently learned Mike wanted to choose an outside candidate for the position I eventually got, but Phil persuaded Mike to give me a chance and even asked our CEO to intervene on behalf of my candidacy. I heard through the grapevine that some people within the company saw this job as Phil's retirement gift to me, which is a load of bull. I earned this job. I deserve it.

When Mike hired me for the position, he seemed very cool, distant, and aloof. I think he resented the pressure he may have been under to select me for this role. Honestly, not having a supportive relationship with my boss has been a bit unnerving for me. It makes me wish for the good old days when Phil was in charge.

Shortly after accepting the position, I shared with Mike my desire to replace our VP of R&D, Dan Arrington, and our VP of Operations, Bob Estes. Arrington is a knowledgeable guy, but didn't strike me as very results-focused. Our Operations head, Bob Estes, was reasonably competent, but had been in the job for fifteen years. He seemed to be only going through the motions and was definitely not a driver. I believed bringing in some outside talent to the division was key, and these were the two positions that would have the most impact on reinvigorating our organization. Shouldn't a divisional president be allowed to make the call on who is on or off his team? Unfortunately for me, Mike didn't quite see it that way and "asked" me to focus on developing stronger relationships with both men and building a more cohesive team for the upcoming year. Only then, he said, could we reevaluate the situation.

I was miffed by Mike's reluctance to support my recommendation and haven't honestly done as much as I could have to build a relationship with either Bob or Dan. Over the past six months, Mike has subtly made it clear that he doesn't perceive the division's performance shortfall as the fault of Operations or R&D. So, getting new players in these roles doesn't seem to be a viable short-term option. I'm stuck with these losers.

When Phil retired, he confided in me that he really did go out on a limb to persuade Mike to offer me the job. Mike was very concerned, and rightfully so, about putting a person in a high-ranking divisional leadership position with no previous general management experience. With our performance shortfall this year, I wonder if I validated Mike's concerns. Has he given up on me? Will he give up on me? I figure I have this coming year to make things right, or I'll be sent packing.

New Year's is just a week away, and right now, I'm just glad to see this awful, stressful year end. We've got a realistic plan for next year, and I'll just turn up the burners on the team to execute. No excuses. Next year will be better and we'll get back on track. For now, though, I'm out of juice and can't wait to kick back and relax over the holidays.

Here's hoping next year is a whole lot better than this year.

CHAPTER THREE

The Gift

Christmas at our house is typically the holiday highlight of the year. Nancy takes care of all of the details, and it comes off without a hitch. As much as we love our lakeside home during the summer months, winter is when it really transforms into a snow-covered wonderland. Just off Gibson's Point, on the western tip of Robinson's Bay in Deephaven, ours is one of the few homes with an unobstructed east-west view. Through the floor-to-ceiling windows in our four-season sunroom, we can see both the sunrise over the bay at dawn and the gorgeous purples and pinks of the sunset overlooking the lower lake at dusk. In winter it's particularly magical, with our Christmas tree framed by the spectacular sunlight that twinkles off the snow-covered lake, stretching nearly as far as we can see in every direction. Lake Minnetonka is a sprawling body of water, more than 100 feet deep in places, with 110 miles of shoreline touching fifteen communities. Under the ice, the water teems with fish, from walleye, bass, and northern pike to muskie, perch, bullheads, and sunfish. Growing up on a farm in southern Minnesota, I'd dreamed my whole life of moving into a spacious house on a lake. It's even more spectacular than I imagined.

Nancy loves the history of the area and says it makes her feel connected to the community and to the people who used to depend on the lake for their livelihoods. "When I close my eyes and listen to the waves lapping against the shore," she told me once, "I can imagine what it must have been like before these houses were here. Before *any* of this was here."

Formed more than ten thousand years ago when the glaciers melted, Lake Minnetonka was discovered by settlers in 1822, but it had been populated by the Dakota Sioux, Cheyenne, Iowa, and Ojibwa people for centuries before the pioneers arrived on its shores. During its heyday in the 1880s and '90s, Lake Minnetonka was a bustling tourist destination, with more than a dozen hotels and resorts, the thriving Big Island Amusement Park, and huge steamboats that could carry up to 2,500 people from one end of the lake to the other.

Those days are gone, but the lake still stands as one of the Twin Cities' most recognizable landmarks and warm-weather destinations. On broiling summer afternoons, it's so packed with watercraft, it's almost as if you could walk from one side of the lake to the other, stepping from boat to boat. Other times of the year, especially during the winter, it seems as remote as a northern Minnesota cabin.

Nancy often sets up her easel in the sunroom and paints as the sun sets over the lake, dabbing at the canvas and trying to capture the view. "I just like to come in here and simply *be,*" she told me once. "It's inspiring." I have a hard time with a statement like that. Is it beautiful? Yes. Calming? Absolutely. But inspirational? I don't see it. Still, I know that Nancy is able to experience a strong sense of calm by just sitting and absorbing the view. It's her favorite room in the house, especially in the winter.

Our fifteen-year-old, Jeff, and thirteen-year-old, Amber, love the season and still act a lot like little kids on Christmas morning. Nancy does most of the shopping, all the decorating, takes care of the cards, and makes sure we all get involved in our long-standing holiday traditions. One of our favorite Christmas customs is what we call "Nicollet Night." Each year, we take the kids to dinner at McCormick & Schmick's on Nicollet Avenue in downtown Minneapolis, where we can see the Holidazzle parade from our table by the window.

There's something very comforting about sitting in a cozy restaurant watching people dressed like giant Christmas tree lights waddle by in subzero temperatures.

Still, I've had some trouble getting into the Christmas mindset this year. I figure it's mostly because of the generally foul mood I've been in thanks to the crummy year I've been having at work. The past few days have been a godsend, and I'm finally getting into the spirit.

I'm going to miss this when it's time to head back to the office.

• • •

We woke up to four inches of snow on a bright, sunny, and cold Minnesota Christmas morning. Christmas Day at our house is totally laid back—just the four of us hanging out in our pajamas with our pet golden retriever, Dakota, enjoying each others' company. Nancy and I decided years ago that Christmas would be for the kids, and so we insist on celebrating in our own home on Christmas Day. We'll visit friends and relatives later.

After watching Dakota romp in the fresh snow, I made the coffee and helped Nancy make our traditional egg casserole. It's Nancy's own recipe, an unbelievable blend of hard-boiled eggs, bacon, and crushed potato chips that gets my mouth watering the second we pull it from the oven. For a lot of people, it's just not Christmas until the turkey, mashed potatoes, and cookies are passed around, but for me, there's nothing like the familiar, comfortable feeling I get as we all sit around the breakfast table and dig into the casserole. Nancy pulled apart strips of bacon and set them in the sizzling pan while I sliced up the eggs.

"When was the last time we did something like this?" she asked, a huge grin on her face. I could barely remember when we'd last taken the time to cook together. Easter? Maybe last Christmas? I wasn't sure. Work has been so all-encompassing, I've had to make some sacrifices along the way, and time with my family was one of the first things that needed to move to the back burner. It was a sacrifice we all needed to make, I knew, while I focused on my job.

After we finished putting the egg casserole together, the four of us exchanged our gifts. Sitting around on Christmas morning, listening to our favorite carols and exchanging our presents made me realize how lucky I was, having this beautiful family. For a moment or two, I also felt a tinge of guilt for not appreciating them more, for being preoccupied at work this past year. I realized that it had undoubtedly been the most painful year of my career, but the sad truth is that I have always spent an inordinate amount of time at work. Often, even when I'm at home, I'm trying to catch up on some paperwork or thinking about the office. My family isn't getting nearly as much of me as they deserve. It was a bittersweet day. On one hand, it was a phenomenal feeling to be so close to Nancy and the kids as we laughed, connected, and just enjoyed being together. But I also realized that when I went back to work, we'd return to our normal routine, and the warm feeling I felt in my stomach would harden back into a heavy ball of tension.

After it looked like we'd opened all our gifts, Nancy arched her eyebrow and said there was one more present for me to open. The kids grew quiet and sat next to us on the sofa. Nancy handed me an envelope, and I got a strong feeling they were all in on the surprise. I opened the envelope and unfolded a one-page brochure the kids had made on our home computer. It read:

Merry Christmas, Dad. You're going on a one-week ski vacation in Vail, Colorado! Love, Nancy, Jeff, and Amber.

"There's more on the back," Amber said, nearly tearing the brochure from my hands. I flipped it over and started to read. Nancy had set me up with a flight directly on Northwest Airlines from the Twin Cities to Vail/Eagle County Airport. She booked a suite for me at the Marriott Mountain Resort and Spa in the Lionshead area of Vail, and she had already arranged equipment rental and lessons with an instructor named Ed Davis. Nancy knew I loved to ski in high school and college. But since graduation, I'd only found time to hit the slopes on a couple of occasions.

"So this is just for me?" I asked.

Nancy nodded. "And we're not taking no for an answer."

They knew, better than anyone, what a strain the past year has been. Nancy, Amber, and Jeff were giving me a "license to chill"—an opportunity to recharge my batteries and enjoy some time alone, reflecting and doing something that was good for me both spiritually and physically. What a family! Still, I was a little nervous about leaving work for a whole week. Vacations, no matter how necessary, were looked upon as a sign of weakness in our company for senior leaders like me. But I'd deal with that later. What was important now was letting my family know how much I appreciated the gesture.

"Thanks a lot," I said, mustering a big smile and taking them all in my arms.

After we cleaned up the torn wrapping paper and the kids went to bed, Nancy and I flopped down on the couch. We sat there for what seemed like hours, watching the bulbs twinkle on the tree. She laid her head on my shoulder, the way she used to before things got tense at work.

"So who's this Ed Davis character?" I finally asked.

"He's supposed to be the best," she said.

"You already pay for the lessons?"

She poked me gently in the ribs. "Why? Do you think you're too good for a refresher course?"

"Well, I do consider myself a pretty competent skier."

"Ben, it's been forever since you've been skiing." She reminded me that more than two decades had flown by since my buddies and I last skied and partied at night in northern Minnesota at Lutsen ski resort. With 3,500 vertical feet and an elevation of more than 11,500 feet, Vail was a different deal, a real Colorado mountain. "And actually," she said, "it's not one lesson; it's five."

"Five?"

"You don't sound too enthused," she said, and I could feel her own enthusiasm beginning to fade.

"It's not that. I just don't think I need an instructor telling me how to put my skis on or how to maneuver down the bunny hill with a bunch of kids with runny noses."

"Dave and Deb Morem recommended the guy," she said, almost defensively. "They hire him for their annual ski trips to Vail, and they're pretty talented skiers. They swear he's a great instructor who inspires care and confidence."

"Sounds fine," I said, and pulled her closer to me. "Really." But, truthfully, I still wasn't convinced. Secretly, I thought it was overkill, a waste of time and money, and decided to talk with her later about scaling back the lessons to one or, at most, two.

I definitely didn't need some hotshot ski bum trying to teach me what I probably already knew.

CHAPTER FOUR

Like Riding a Bike

The Christmas break was excellent—lots of relaxation and good times with family and friends, and plenty of food and drink. Nancy says I watched too much football, which was a rare treat. Most days off, I'm barricaded in my home office, struggling to catch up on a never-ending pile of reports. This week, though, I planted myself in front of the TV and enjoyed every minute of it.

I was getting more excited about my ski trip to Vail. We confirmed the dates and details, and, though I was still reluctant, Nancy convinced me to keep the ski lessons.

In an effort to find my ski legs, Nancy and I took a couple of days to ski at Spirit Mountain in Duluth while our neighbors watched the kids. Nancy can take or leave skiing, but she was a good sport, and it was fun for me to get back out on skis after a hiatus of twenty years or so. Ski equipment had sure changed a lot! The new parabolic skis we tried were short and fat, sort of shaped like an hourglass, but they did make it easy to turn. The good news is that skiing is somewhat like riding a bike—once you learn, you never forget. I'm a little older and a lot less flexible than I used to be, but I got the hang of it in no time and even skied some of the advanced, black diamond runs by the end of the second day. And I handled them just fine, if I do say so myself.

But all the while I was on the slopes, I dreaded what awaited me at the end of my time off—work.

CHAPTER FIVE

Back to Work

On Tuesday morning I reluctantly headed back to the office. We held our bi-weekly GSLT meeting. Our chief financial officer, Miguel Hernandez, ran through the final sales numbers and our preliminary bottom line. Thanks to the extra effort by our head of sales, Craig Peters, and his team, we had a strong December and actually were going to finish just 5 percent off our sales plan number. It's still not a good thing to miss the budget, I knew, but 5 percent away is better than 7 percent. Miguel reported that we would cut down our miss on the operating profit number, too. Again, we can't have two years in a row where we miss plan, but I appreciated the effort and hoped we'd be able to leverage that momentum to propel us into the first few months of the new year.

Dan Arrington, our head of R&D, updated us on the progress of our new products, including *CyberLaser*, our new laser surgical device we're betting heavily on this year. He said that because tests at a select group of hospitals were going well, everything was on track for the national launch of *CyberLaser* by March 1. Even though the product had been delayed twice before it finally hit the testing phase, 70 percent of our planned sales growth this coming year is based on what we believe will be a successful launch for this product and its family of accessories. We've built into the operating plan to convert our existing customers from our old *Conquistador* family to the new *CyberLaser* family, as well as convert a number of accounts that are served by our competitors. It won't be a slam dunk by any stretch of the imagination, but we can do it if these guys work together and execute. A successful launch and conversion is an absolute must if we are to meet and exceed this year's plan.

Bob Estes, who leads Operations, discussed the ramp-up required for the *CyberLaser* launch. To gain cost efficiencies, we're relying heavily on producers of sub-components from Asia, and the final product will be assembled by two contract outfits in Mexico. The build-up is on schedule and Bob promises we'll have enough units to meet our forecast for launch in March. I'm nervous because we're relying heavily on outside, foreign vendors over which we have little control. But I'm holding Bob accountable.

Craig Peters gave us an update of the upcoming national sales meeting in Orlando. There will be two messages our sales management and sales representatives will leave with: First, we missed plan last year and that can't happen this year; and second, the flawless launch of *CyberLaser* and snatching away competitive accounts will be key. We truly believe *CyberLaser* is a game-changing product. And we're going to give the sales people a chance to earn a significant spiff for converting competitive accounts.

Our VP of Human Resources, Denise Washington, updated us on our new benefit plan enrollment statistics and the status of our recent hiring activity. After the meeting, she told me that I would have the results of my 360-degree feedback early next week. *Just great*, I thought. CardMedics is conducting a pilot 360-degree process for its top twenty executives. The assessments were conducted in December, and I'll get feedback from Mike, my direct reports, and a few others in the organization. Given what we went through last year, I'm not exactly looking forward to any feedback from, or reminders of, the past year. Even in good times, I'm not a particularly reflective guy and prefer to focus on the present and future. I do need to be a good soldier, though, as Mike was a proponent of the assessment process, and I'll be required to follow up with him on key points brought up in the process. Really looking forward to that discussion. Not!

That night I dreamed that Mike was chasing me down a ski hill, a 360-degree report in one hand and a pink slip in the other.

CHAPTER SIX

Painful Feedback

I received my 360-degree feedback report today. As I mentioned, this is a pilot process and in retrospect, I wish I would have insisted my direct reports be assessed, too. They completed the assessment in mid-December, when we were at a low point, and I think the timing and the pressure my staff felt may have skewed the results. The findings weren't exactly surprising. I know from the sports teams I've been on that there's always a lot of complaining when the team is losing. This situation was no exception. I wish I had the opportunity to rate each of my direct reports, too, as they did with me.

My direct reports tore me apart—low marks on self-awareness, low empathy toward others, and my relationship skills were rated as "needs improvement." From Mike, I received a requirement to be "more committed to achieving results through others," to "use more effective leadership styles," and to "create a more positive working climate" among my direct reports. I wondered how Mike knew about the climate? And more important, why should he care? How I get the results, as long as it's not done illegally, shouldn't be any of his concern.

On the positive side of the ledger, they all commented on my high level of self-confidence and smarts. Given last year, I'm not so certain about either the confidence or the smarts anymore, but it was nice to hear.

Some of the verbatim comments at the end of the report really stung. A few of the more memorable were:

- "Ben has not proven he is able to effectively bring an executive team together."
- "The hub-and-spoke management style isn't conducive to real teamwork. We don't debate issues as a team—only with Ben. He's the Lone Ranger. This may have worked well when he was a marketing head, but it doesn't work for an executive team when he's the president of our division."
- "With Ben, you are guilty until proven innocent."
- "Ben's dominant leadership styles are directive and turning up the pace. No vision, no motivation, no coaching, no meaningful participation."
- "Ben uses people to gain results; he doesn't really see us as people, but more like tools."

Ouch! Receiving this feedback was obviously not a lot of fun. I acknowledge that relationship skills are not my strong suit, but come on—these are high-priced, experienced executives, and they should be able to do their jobs without a lot of coddling. When they need help from one another, they should ask for it and not depend on me to have a crystal ball and play referee whenever they need to work through an issue with a peer. I've never felt a lot of need for praise and recognition, so why do these people need it? Can't they motivate themselves? And what's with them claiming I don't have any vision?

While there are some areas I'd be willing to improve as a leader, this 360-degree pilot process didn't provide for any follow-up assistance or guidance. I think this is a mistake. After all, it's easy to criticize, but here's a thought: give me some suggestions for improvement if that's what is needed. I'm sure Mike will have some ideas about all of this when I speak with him about the results on Friday.

CHAPTER SEVEN

The Ultimatum

Well, I met with Mike today. He read my assessment report, and as I feared, he certainly did have some ideas. "Missing plan is never acceptable," he said as he paced around his office, barely looking me in the eye. "There may be extenuating circumstances that once in a decade would excuse a near miss, but as far as I can tell, there were no extenuating circumstances this year." He stopped and sat at the edge of his desk, exhaling deeply. "From my perspective we missed because of poor execution and leadership. If there's another miss this year, you're not going to be around for a third try."

As I sat there in silence and let his words sink in, he kept tossing verbal darts, hitting deeper and deeper. "And I'm very concerned about the working climate you've created with your leadership team. The 360-degree results corroborate the anecdotal feedback I've been hearing for almost a year."

"What kind of feedback?" I said, my throat dry.

"You're not pulling together your team to work through problems. Instead, I hear you're grabbing one or two of the individual team members to work the issues with you."

I felt a sense of betrayal and my face reddened with anger. This revelation confirmed that Estes and Arrington were feeding Mike information about me and the team. I recalled my earlier discussion with Mike, and I wished I'd been more insistent in getting rid of these guys and putting in new players I could trust. They stabbed me in the back.

Bottom line, Mike told me I needed improvement on two fronts for the coming year. In addition to meeting the plan for the year, he was requiring me to be a more inclusive leader by improving the working climate for my direct reports. "Any shortfall in either the results or these behaviors," Mike stated with an almost eerie calmness, "would require a top leadership change."

As I left Mike's office, I felt some powerful, mixed emotions. On one hand, it was crystal clear that we have to win this year. We're in full agreement, and I accept that requirement. On the other hand, his ultimatum to become a more inclusive leader and improve the climate on the GSLT seemed subjective and of lesser importance. Third, I felt betrayed by some members of my team.

If we had made plan, would Mike be requiring me to make these changes in behavior? I doubt it. One thing was for sure: we'd better perform or I'm out the door. And if that happens, I'll make damn sure I'm not the only one.

CHAPTER EIGHT

Rallying the Troops

We just finished our three-day sales meeting in Orlando, and I spent a total of about ten minutes in the gorgeous Florida sun, mostly as I walked from meetings on one side of the resort to the other. We were inundated with training seminars and meetings on the *CyberLaser* launch. I gave the speech at dinner on the second night about the need to recommit to performance this coming year, and I think I ended up coming off as kind of a jerk. I made it clear about my disappointment in our sales shortfall last year.

Before it finally launched, *CyberLaser* had been delayed six months as a result of R&D issues. The delay wasn't the sales managers' fault, but I was disappointed in them nonetheless. Isn't it the job of sales management to pick up the slack so we always make our plan? Some of the managers let us down by not driving their teams hard enough.

I know it was difficult to receive, but I felt I had no choice but to deliver a tough, clear, and direct message. My speech definitely put a damper on the evening; you could feel the energy just drain from the room. Fortunately, we hired a comedian to entertain the crowd following my dinner speech. He poked a little good-natured fun at me, the crowd roared with delight, the drinks started flowing, and the evening was soon upbeat again.

As usual, and in stark contrast to my downer of a speech, Craig did a great job as Master of Ceremonies for the meeting. He balanced the message of not being satisfied with last year's performance with the need to make sure the *CyberLaser* launch was flawless.

Craig is the consummate national sales manager. He's professional, a great motivator, optimistic with a can-do attitude, an excellent coach of his people, respected by customers, and an "A" player in every sense of the definition. I sense our sales team is embracing the new *CyberLaser* product family and is really behind our efforts, and I'd bet a good portion of that confidence is directly attributable to Craig.

Almost sixty, Craig had been the head of sales for the Cardiac Rhythm Management business for years, prior to his retirement four years ago. Craig and I worked closely together for five years when I headed Marketing for that division. When I took over at General Surgery and our VP of Sales was named to a new role in International shortly thereafter, I asked Craig to consider joining me for a few years. By that time, Craig had played enough golf and said that, sure, he would take the job and stay as long as it was fun. Last year was certainly not fun, but the pro that he is, I know Craig will break his butt to make the *CyberLaser* launch a success and help us make the year. I figure Craig has enough gas in his tank for two or three more years.

More than anyone else on the leadership team, I depend on Craig. He's everything I'm not—compassionate, empathetic, upbeat.

Frankly, I don't know what I'd do without him.

CHAPTER NINE

A Black and White Message

I want to tell myself the timing was just coincidental.

Mike just circulated an article from the *Twin Cities Business Journal* to his staff that includes two other divisional presidents, Mike's CFO, and the head of HR. The title of the article was "Top Reasons for Executive Derailment." While he distributed it to his entire staff, I couldn't help but think that after our review of last week, he was sending me a public message. I read the article four times. Three of the top five reasons for derailment, as described in the article, concern me greatly: Failure to build partnerships with peers and subordinates; failure to make two to three critical objectives; and failure to learn the new job quickly enough.

Honestly, it seems Mike had this article printed for my benefit. It might have well been accompanied by a big picture of me with a target painted on my head. The other guys have been in their roles for quite awhile and are making plan. They seem to get along great with Mike. I feel as if Mike is sending me a message, and there's no doubt in my mind that my peers now know he's singling me out, too.

I leave for Vail on Sunday, and I'm torn. On one hand, it's been years since I've taken a week off work, and this might be as good a time as any to get away. January looks to be a decent month from a sales standpoint. We just completed a successful national sales meeting, and Mike was clear with me about his expectations for the year. Our new product launch is on track, and we have a chance to have an excellent year with hard work and some lucky breaks. Maybe I'll be able to leave town and relax, knowing that things are under control. Or at least confident that things won't get any worse while I'm gone.

On the other hand, we're coming off a tough year and taking some time off now could raise some eyebrows. But as much as I don't want to disappoint my boss, I want to disappoint Nancy and the kids even less. They seemed so excited when they gave me the gift; more than anybody, they understand how much I could use some time away from the office. Who knows—maybe it'll be exactly what I need.

I eventually decided that even though I'd probably be thinking about work the whole time I was gone, a trip now would help me prepare for the grueling upcoming twelve months. CardMedics will still be there when I get back. I know what needs to be done. We're going to have a challenging year, and I need to take some time to unwind—and gear up for the issues ahead of me.

CHAPTER TEN

A Sudden Loss

On Saturday morning, the day before I was to leave for Vail, I got a distressing call from Craig asking if he could meet with me in person for an important discussion. We agreed to get together at the Caribou Coffee in the Lake Minnetonka community of Wayzata at 2:00 p.m.

Looking out at the ice fishing shanties on Wayzata Bay, Craig swirled the coffee in his cup. "I'm leaving, Ben."

My mouth opened, but no words came out.

"It was a tough decision, but I need to go." He looked at me, and the usual spark in his eyes was somehow gone. "Effective as soon as possible."

I felt my heart beat faster. It was as if my security blanket had just unraveled into a pile of thread. I ran my hands through my hair. "How come?"

He smiled. "They were going to revoke my golf membership at Wayzata Country Club for lack of use."

"Come on," I said. "You and I both know that's not the reason."

He paused, and took a sip of his coffee. "It's you."

"Me?"

"I would never criticize you in the 360-degree process, but I need to share some things with you."

I nodded and felt as if I had been hit by a bus.

"You're a changed man from our time together at Cardiac Rhythm Management, Ben. I'm your biggest supporter on the GSLT, but everyone pretty much feels like you're in it just for you. They say you're treating them as things to be used, and no one is engaged the way you'd like them to be."

"And you," I finally said. "Is that how you feel, too?"

He nodded slowly. "I'm out of gas, too. It's been a struggle. And rather than work in a situation that leaves a lot to be desired, after a lot of careful thought, I decided it's time to get on with my retirement."

"I see." My last supporter was bailing on me.

"Sorry for dropping this on you just before you head out of town, but I feel I owe it to you to shoot straight and share the news with you as soon as possible."

"Oh, man," I said, suddenly realizing what it would mean to our business. "The *CyberLaser* launch."

"Yeah, I thought a lot about that, too. I know how important it is. I'm willing to stay on to help. How about we make my last day June 30, the end of the second quarter? That should give us enough time to make sure *CyberLaser* launches the way it should."

I mustered a smile and thanked Craig for sticking with me until the end of the quarter and for sharing the difficult news with me in a classy way.

Professional that he is, Craig seemed to read my mind, and he suggested we meet again following my ski vacation to work through the details, including the right time to communicate to Mike and the team. Again, I thanked him for his thoughtfulness during what was a devastating moment for me. As I watched him walk out the door, one thought echoed through my head: *Is working with me really that bad?*

I returned home to finish packing, but the enthusiasm of the past twenty-four hours was nowhere to be found. The air was definitely out of the balloon.

• • •

Before being away from them for a week, I planned to take my family out for a night of fun. We went to downtown Minneapolis for burgers at Ike's and then made the short walk through the skyway to the Target Center, where we watched the Minnesota Timberwolves host the Denver Nuggets. Kevin Garnett had a classic "KG night," scoring twenty-five points, pulling down fifteen rebounds, and gaining ten assists—yet another triple-double night. Wally Sczerbiak pitched in with twenty-one points as the Wolves schooled talented, young Carmello Anthony and his supporting cast 105 to 93.

Still, as much as I enjoyed the game, I couldn't help but feel a pang of jealousy as I watched Garnett. He was as gifted as any single player in the game today, dominating the court with his talent and confidence. But while he made an incredible impact as an individual, he also knew how to work effectively with his team. He recognized that even though his teammates might not be as talented as he is, they all had their strengths, and they all had something to contribute. He didn't hot dog it through the whole game, stepping over his team-mates to make a basket. He passed the ball. He set picks. He acted like they were a team.

I wondered what was wrong with me that I couldn't get my reports at the office to work together to get the job done. Was I that ineffective as a leader? As I watched the Wolves fly up and down the court, passing the ball back and forth like a well-oiled machine, I worried about Craig's decision to leave and the impact that would have on the sales force, the GSLT, and, most importantly, me.

"You seem like you're not even here," my son Jeff said. "What's wrong?"

I shook my head and tried to deflect his question, pretending to watch the game.

He slumped in his seat. "Looks like we're seeing a repeat of last year's Dad."

That comment made me put extra effort into ignoring the gnawing feeling in my gut and making the night a fun one. I touched him on the shoulder and gave him a smile. "Sorry, Kiddo. Just dealing with some work stuff. I'll set it aside."

"Promise?"

I nodded. "Promise." As if on cue, Garnett leaped into the air and dunked the ball, hanging from the rim as the crowd exploded in a frenzy of cheers.

To celebrate the T-Wolves' victory, we went to the Block E entertainment complex after the game, got dessert at the Hard Rock Cafe, and played video games at GameWorks. The kids and Nancy had a really good time. I acted like I did, too, but my mind was someplace else.

There were thousands of people all around me, but I felt completely alone.

CHAPTER ELEVEN

The Phone Call

The muted Minnesota sunlight shone through our bedroom window. It was a new day. Thank God. I wiped the sleep from my eyes and reminded myself that no executive is irreplaceable. Craig will work with me to ensure a smooth transition, and as disappointing as his departure is, we should be okay. At least, that's what I told myself. He'll leave a considerable hole when he goes. He is an excellent developer of people and I've long admired his talent in this area. But Craig has a capable lieutenant, Lisa Armstrong, who will be an internal candidate to fill the role. As much as I'll miss Craig, we'll get through it. It's not going to be easy, though.

Just before the limo arrived to take me to the Minneapolis-St. Paul International Airport, I kissed Nancy and the kids goodbye and reminded myself to enjoy the week and relax. But it was tough to let go. During the ninety-minute flight to Eagle and the short Colorado Express van ride to Vail, my mind replayed everything that had fallen on me over the past few days. I knew I needed to come up with a new game plan while I was in Vail. I arrived at the Marriott in Lionshead by 1:00 p.m., exhausted from reliving my crummy week again and again.

Rather than ski, I decided to check in, pick up my rental equipment at Charter Sports, get in a quick workout and lunch, and check out Vail Village and Lionshead. Vail is absolutely breathtaking. When I arrived at the hotel, it was thirty-five degrees and sunny, without a cloud in the sky. The air was dry, and with the sun and no wind, it actually felt much, much warmer than what the thermometer read. The weather was a great break from Minnesota's gray, deep freeze of a winter.

When I returned to my suite after dinner at Los Amigos in Vail Village, there was an urgent message from Dan Arrington waiting for me. No details on the message, which made me nervous. If it was good news, he would have said a lot more than, "Ben, it's Dan. Call me at home as soon as you get this. Doesn't matter how late."

I stood by the window and dialed his home number. He picked up on the first ring, as if he was sitting by the phone, waiting for me to call. His voice was clenched and thin.

"You sitting down?" he said, and I felt my stomach drop.

"Just spill it, Dan," I said, closing my eyes and concentrating on keeping calm.

"It's *CyberLaser*. We've got a problem."

I sat down.

"It's the results we're getting from the pre-launch evaluations." Dan told me that in the past week, we'd received complaints on malfunctions of the *CyberLaser* from three locations that are testing the new system: the Cleveland Clinic, the University of Minnesota, and Baylor's M.D. Anderson Cancer Clinic in Houston. As Dan's team investigated the complaints, they discovered a software snafu that somehow caused the unit to short out after it had been used continuously for twenty minutes.

"Twenty minutes," I repeated softly, convinced that he had to be mistaken. It's not uncommon for surgeries to take three hours or longer, and a problem like this one, if we couldn't quickly fix it, could be a show stopper. "Jesus, Dan. You're telling me that they've got someone laid out on the operating table and the laser shorts out?"

Dan breathed deeply. "That's what I'm telling you. And it gets even worse. Softwrite Design Partners, the software developer we hired for the work, is facing bankruptcy."

"Don't you mean the software developer *you* hired?" I snapped.

Dan was silent on the other end of the line, then cleared his throat. "That's right. The developer *I* hired. I talked to Softwrite's acting president right before I left the message for you."

"How could this have happened?" I asked, shaking my head. "Softwrite's done good work for us over the years. Please tell me they're on this."

Silence again. "He says given their situation, they're focusing all their energies on keeping the company afloat. They're down to a skeleton staff; they laid just about everybody off while they figure out how to move forward. Our account manager is no longer with the company," Dan sighed. "Bottom line: he's not optimistic they'll be of much help at this point."

My shock turned to anger, and I stood and began pacing around the hotel room. "Do we have any performance provisions in our contract with Softwrite? Could we withhold payment as leverage to get the problem fixed?"

Dan paused, inhaled loudly, and told me that he'd already okayed the final software. "It worked perfectly in our internal testing and first-phase trials before we shipped it. Softwrite was paid in full two months ago."

"What are you saying to me? We have no recourse?" Both my blood pressure and voice rose. Contractually, they had filled their obligation to us.

Dan explained that we had executed our contract with Softwrite when Jean Flemming, our general counsel, was on medical leave. We were on such an aggressive schedule, neither Jean nor one of our corporate attorneys had reviewed the agreement before Dan signed it. In fact, it was little more than Softwrite's boilerplate contract, so of course, there were no performance provisions in their version.

"Let me see if I've got this straight," I said. I knew Dan could hear every bit of the tension in my voice, and I didn't care. "We paid Softwrite almost $3.5 million for software that now appears to be, at best, flawed and, at worst, worthless. We had no assurance they were willing or able to fix any problems that arose, and now we've got no legal recourse. What's worse, we have a new product launch in thirty days, the success of which will make or break our year. Am I on the right track here, Dan? Do I have it right?"

"Yeah," he said softly. "You've got it right."

I breathed deeply and worked to calm the jackhammer in my chest. "What are you doing to fix this?"

"I'm flying to San Francisco in the morning to personally meet with Softwrite's acting president. I'm going to do everything possible to persuade him, and if necessary, threaten and even beg them to fix the problem. My new product development team is also scrambling to find other software developers as a backup plan."

"That's something," I said, running my hand over my hair. "But even if Softwrite is willing and able to solve the problem, we're still looking at a delay, right?"

"Depending on how long a fix will take and given our two-month buildup of inventory units, which, depending on the fix, will now either need to be scrapped or re-worked, we'll be looking at at least a three-month delay. Maybe as much as six to nine months if new software needs to be written." Dan paused. "We also face the added expense of re-working or scrapping two months of production and the lost sales of three to nine months of new product revenue."

Upon hearing Dan's response, I took a deep breath and then launched into a profanity-filled rant I cannot repeat. "I'm profoundly disappointed, Dan," I said. This was a massive display of utter incompetence on his behalf, a total lack of management of the contract, vendor, and software validation process. My voice was like cold steel. "This is the second delay we've had with *CyberLaser*. You and your team really screwed up. You're going to have a plan to fix the problem in twenty-four hours," I said. "I expect a call no later than 9:00 p.m. Monday with the new game plan."

Dan's voice trembled on the line. "I'm sorry, Ben. I'll do the best I can to fix this. I'll do everything I can."

"Do you realize this division's performance for the year, not to mention your career at CardMedics, is riding on how you recover on this problem *you* created?"

"Yes, Ben," he said, feebly.

"Call me tomorrow!" I shouted as I slammed down the receiver and swore as loudly as I could. At that moment I felt simultaneously sick to my stomach and full of rage. Dan's management of this fiasco was absolutely and categorically incompetent. Even if he could somehow pull a rabbit out of his hat and get this problem fixed quickly, he's got to go, I thought. If we have a delay of three months or more, the party's over. We won't make our number and my career at CardMedics will be history.

Skiing was the last thing on my mind, and I debated leaving Vail immediately. I checked the Northwest website—the next flight home wasn't until Monday evening. *Dammit*, I thought. *What in the world am I doing in Vail when my life is crumbling?* Over the past thirty-six hours my top performer resigned, my business fell into shambles, this year's plan was going down the toilet, and my career at CardMedics was hanging by a rapidly unraveling thread.

What could I do? I decided to do the only thing I could do—reduce my stress. I started the ten-minute walk to Vail Village and paced through town in an effort to calm myself down. Steam was coming out of my ears, I think. When I get under the gun, self-control has never been my strong suit. It's a good thing I was out of town and not face-to-face with Dan, or I probably would have said or done some things that might come back to haunt me. I was already hard on the guy, but I didn't care. He needed to understand just how much he'd screwed up. And if I bruised his feelings in the process, so be it.

A few blocks from the mountain in the Village, I heard live music coming out of The Red Lion. I walked in, sat down, listened to the band, and slammed a few drinks to drown my troubles. Three hours and several martinis later, I stumbled into a cab, found my room at the Marriott, and passed out.

CHAPTER TWELVE

The Wipeout

The alarm beeped at 5:00 a.m. I woke up groggy with a severe case of cottonmouth and a screaming head, the result of too much alcohol consumed at a high altitude, dry mountain air, and too much bad news. I stumbled into the bathroom to get a glass of water and to swallow pain reliever for my aching head. On the way back to bed, I peeked through the curtains and noticed we'd been hit by a snowstorm that looked to have dumped several inches of powder. I would have been thoroughly charged with the fresh dump of snow a couple of days ago, but the news about *CyberLaser* dampened my enthusiasm toward snow or skiing.

What are my options? I thought. *What should I do?* As I thought it through, I decided to make no decisions until I heard from Dan that night. Except one. I was going to fire Dan as soon as I returned to Minneapolis.

I've never wanted Dan on my team; he's known that, I thought. He stabbed me in the back with Mike and now it was time to for him to pay with his career. I decided to put Bob in charge of both R&D and Operations and work very closely with him as we implement our recovery plan. Can Bob make it work? Who knows? But he's going to get the chance, and I planned to be his shadow the next several months.

I considered calling an ad hoc meeting of all our division's vice presidents and directors the week of my return to discuss the *CyberLaser* launch and let Dan explain the situation he put us in. That would be embarrassing for Dan, and it would allow this group of thirty leaders to hear the real story. I then decided I would fire him that night following the special meeting. I thought about how good it would feel when Dan was gone. Firing him would be a wakeup call to those in the division who think I don't take performance seriously.

To make this plan work, I'd have to brief Mike and get him in my corner to let Dan go. *This is showtime*, I thought. If Mike didn't support me on this move, I didn't see how I'd be able to continue in my role.

After three extra-strength Excedrin, breakfast at the Marriott's cafe, and several cups of coffee, I returned to my room to check my e-mail and voicemail. Nothing from Dan, but I didn't expect anything until later. I checked in with Nancy to let her know about my latest bit of bad news, and to tell her that I'd be heading home early.

"Ben, I know you're upset, but there's no reason to leave," she said quickly.

"Excuse me?"

"You heard me. Like it or not, you *need* to stick it out in Vail."

"Look," I said, slumping onto the bed. "I know it's an expensive trip, and, believe me, I feel badly about cutting it short. But—"

"It has nothing to do with the money. If you hop on that plane, you're going to undo any tiny bit of relaxation you've managed to experience during the trip. Think about it logically. There's absolutely nothing you can do from here that you can't do from your hotel room, right? Make calls, get calls, check email?"

"Right, but—"

"No buts," she said. "Like it or not, you need to stay. I can hear how panicked you are, but your judgment's cloudy. Stay there, babe. Doctor's orders."

She was right. She usually was. Since the day we met, Nancy had exhibited an unbelievable knack for saving me from myself. If I was working too hard in the backyard, she insisted I take a break. If I was stressed about a problem at the office, she'd talk through it with me. She knew me, maybe even better than I knew myself. Throughout our marriage, the only times I really found myself painted into a corner were the times I disregarded her advice. I valued her input, and she knew it. She could help me see the big picture better than anybody.

"I hear you," I said. "Look, I'm too worked up about this to commit to sticking it out the whole week. But here's a compromise: How about I ski today and Tuesday, then play it by ear? There's a 6:20 flight out of here on Tuesday night. That'll give me a minimum of two days to ski and relax. And if I'm still stressed out then, I'll head home."

"Sounds like a good start," she said. "Just so you know, though, I'll try to talk you out of leaving then, too."

"I figured you would," I said smiling.

We talked some more about how the last few days had been for her and the kids, and said goodbye. I set the phone down and took a deep breath, admiring the breathtaking view outside my hotel room window.

I got my ski stuff on to tackle the day.

· · ·

I stepped off the Eagle Bahn gondola just after 9:00 a.m., inhaling the mountain air and feeling it clear my muddled head. I figured I had the morning to get familiar with some of the enormous Vail Mountain terrain before hooking up with my instructor after lunch. Now that I was on the mountain, I was eager to hit the slopes. Vail has nearly 200 runs and almost 5,300 skiable acres, and before I got the news from Dan, I had wanted to ski every inch of the place. By 9:20 a.m., I was standing at the top of Born Free, a blue intermediate run I hoped would be an excellent, fun warm-up for the day. The sun peeked out from behind the clouds and illuminated a gorgeous vista, with the mountain covered in eight inches of light, sparkling powder.

It still felt a bit foreign to have skis back on after not having skied in twenty years —with the exception of my quick weekend in Northern Minnesota. I took a deep breath and decided it was too beautiful a run to let my lack of recent experience spoil the morning. I dug my poles into the snow and pushed off into the fresh powder.

As I'd hoped, I slid right back into the groove, embracing the rush of the moment. It was just like riding a bike, only a million times more exhilarating. After returning up the mountain on the Born Free Express, the high-speed detachable quad chair lift that runs alongside the Eagle Bahn gondola, I took an easy snow cat trail to the Avanti Express chair that transported me higher up the mountain. I skied the green novice trail called The Meadows to the Mountain Top Express, the chair lift that carried me to an elevation of 11,250 feet and a spectacular view of snow-covered Vail Valley. It was breathtaking.

I noticed I was huffing and puffing a bit more up here. They warn you to take it easy the first day of skiing at the high altitudes. Rule number one is to watch your alcohol intake, a rule I had already violated. Rule number two is to get a good warm-up on the runs lower on the mountain. But I figured that even though I didn't spend too much time on the easier runs, my instincts would soon take over, and I'd do just fine on the tougher slopes.

Memories of crazy skiing with my college buddies twenty years before entered my mind. I let my thoughts drift, and found myself missing the young man I used to be, the one who didn't let the rigors of life get in his way. What happened to that guy who pushed the limits? Where did he go? The guy who used to take big jumps, schuss aggressively from the top to the bottom of the ski hill, and ski moguls with a reckless disregard for his body? Did I still have it? I decided it was time to find out.

I skied down First Step, then worked my way to Northstar and Log Chute, all advanced black diamond runs, reveling in the wind on my face and the feeling of unbridled freedom I hadn't felt in a long, long time. It took me about twenty minutes to get to the next chair, but I controlled my speed, traversed the slope, and made it down the runs that took me to mid-mountain with only one spill. These runs hadn't been groomed, but I convinced myself that, with all of the soft new snow, it wouldn't be a big deal if I took a tumble. There weren't a lot of people out on that Monday morning, and I told myself I could handle the black runs.

I wouldn't win any style points with my rusty ski form, but I felt a rush of pride and adrenaline with my accomplishment. I celebrated by listening to *Born to Be Wild* by Steppenwolf on my MP3 player. This song was a favorite of mine, one we used to listen to in my buddy's '72 Dodge van on our way to the local Minnesota ski areas. I felt indestructible.

There was still a little of my younger self left in me after all.

The lift to my right as I finished Log Chute was called Highline Lift. I hopped on the chair and it led me to double black diamond, expert-only country. *What the heck?* I thought. *I made it down the black, so I can do the double black, too.* As I considered the double blacks, my memory flashed back to the late '70s when my buddies and I would build gnarly jumps and try to get as much air as possible.

As I got off the lift, I turned to my left and decided to try a double black run named Blue Ox. I took the Blue Ox as a lucky sign. Paul Bunyan, the famous lumberjack of folklore, and his blue ox, Babe, have huge statues in their honor in Northern Minnesota. As a Minnesotan, I thought there was certain symmetry with my choosing Blue Ox versus the other double blacks I could have accessed, like Highline or Roger's Run. So it was off to Blue Ox I went. The next song on my MP3 playlist was AC/DC's *Highway to Hell*—a song that would turn out to be apropos for the situation I was getting myself into. The Blue Ox was about to gore me.

As I was about to find out, so much for symmetry.

I scooted off the lift, paused at the flat terrain at the top of the hill, and overlooked the run. The beginnings of the Blue Ox seemed placid enough, with its fresh powder and borders of evergreens, but looks can be deceiving. I squinted to get a better view. Beyond the first 200 yards of gently sloped terrain, I could make out increasingly steep pitches, peppered with tall, blue, artificial bamboo poles that warned of rocky terrain. If I just stayed away from the exposed rock and stuck to the powder, I'd be fine, I knew. I didn't want to imagine what could happen if I strayed into the exposed rocks.

I took a deep breath, then let gravity take over.

The second I pushed off, I had a terrifying realization. I immediately discovered I had vastly overestimated my skiing capability, and I was totally out of my league. While I worked to avoid the rocky terrain, I completely misjudged the rest of the run. Steep drops and moguls covered by deep powder soon told me unequivocally and unforgivably that I was in the wrong place. Dorothy's line from the *Wizard of Oz*, "Toto, I don't think we're in Kansas anymore," echoed through my head. *God help me*, I thought. *I'm not a twenty-year-old at Lutsen any more.*

I stumbled through the run like a drunken sailor would navigate a street in Shanghai. Midway down I found myself in a steep chute, picking up speed where I had no room to turn. As I accelerated, I realized I needed to veer quickly to my left or run the risk of skiing out of bounds into what appeared to be a ravine. My speed was too high; I was out of control. I leaned to my left and felt my legs waver.

What happened next, I barely remember.

My left ski wobbled and dug itself into the snow, jerking my body forward at an alarming speed. I felt my other leg twist, my right ski flicking wildly against the powder as I spun, then releasing from my boot and hurling through the Colorado sky. And then I was airborne, too, tumbling down the mountain. I let go of my poles and felt my legs fly into the air, then skidded across the snow like a smooth rock on a waveless lake. My arms thrashed against the powder as I fell, and I scrabbled for anything I could grab to help slow my descent. I winced as I made contact with the mountain again, then just as quickly launched into the air, turned what seemed to be a flip, and skittered over the slick snow. Huge stretches of white rushed by me, trees were a green and black blur. I heard myself grunting and gasping for breath as I smashed into the slope again and again. My skis spun off my boots, and I launched into the air once more.

I remember seeing the snow-covered mountain flying toward my face, and then, nothing.

When I came to, there was only total darkness and silence. I felt wet and cold on my face and neck, down my back, and on my hands and wrists. I groaned and slowly shook off the grogginess, remembering I was somewhere on a ski mountain. As I regained my senses, I realized I'd taken the spill of a lifetime. I raised my head slightly to find myself lying face down in a pile of snow. I began taking inventory of my body. My heart was pounding like a drum, and I was having trouble breathing from the snow I inhaled. But while I felt a dull soreness in my back, it didn't seem like any body parts were missing or broken.

A skier in his early twenties schussed over to me and asked, "Dude, are you okay? That was a wicked wipeout! You were doing cartwheels."

I slowly rose to my knees and managed to tell the kid I was okay. He laughed as he skied off. As I looked around, I saw that I'd created a huge pile of snow with my fall. I had just survived the Wipeout of all Wipeouts. The skier who careened down the mountain on the opening of ABC's *Wide World of Sports* had nothing on me.

I had truly experienced the agony of defeat.

I found one ski about fifty feet to my left and caught sight of my poles—one lay near the ski, the other was sticking out of a drift one hundred feet up the mountain. I labored up the slope to gather my equipment, but couldn't find my other ski. The amount of snow that had been displaced by my out-of-control wipeout made it look like a truck had just four-wheeled across the mountain.

To my right was the ravine with its steep and deep drop-off marked by aspen trees and off-limits signs and a very flimsy snow fence. *Thank God for this huge dump of snow*, I thought. *If this had been hard pack or ice, I would have been in that ravine.*

I spent the next forty-five minutes looking for my lost ski. I searched up, over, and down, and couldn't find it. It soon became apparent that thanks to the combination of my high-speed cartwheeling and the deep snow, my ski was buried deep somewhere on the bloody mountain. A couple of skiers stopped to assist me in poking through the deep powder in an effort to find it, but we came up empty. Nothing. Nada.

I remembered my 1:30 p.m. ski lesson, and I cursed the mountain. If there's one thing you need for ski lessons, it's skis. Reluctantly, I came to the conclusion that the damn ski wasn't going to be found until spring.

I pushed the thought from my head and concentrated on getting to the bottom of the mountain. Ski boots were not designed for hiking down a steep slope, especially not high up Vail Mountain. As I made the humiliating march down, I saw skiers on the chair lift staring, pointing, and laughing at me. Total embarrassment. Thirty minutes of walking down a steep slope meant for skiing, not hiking in boots with little to no forward flex, was thirty minutes too many. Even though I was going downhill, because of the deep snow, steep terrain, and high altitude, it was an exhausting, painful hike.

I was sweating profusely, really huffing and puffing. My shins were screaming from the pounding they took from the front of my ski boots. The exhilarating feeling of speeding down the mountain was gone, replaced by the dull ache of despair and self-doubt. I started to think about work again. The experience seemed a bit surreal. I could barely believe I was hiking down a mountain with the current events of my life vividly careening through my mind. All I could think about were all the things that weren't working for me.

My emotions began to overwhelm me. I shook my head at the stupidity of skiing on a double black diamond run. What was I thinking? Totally reckless. I had no business on that run and could have been seriously hurt. I thought about my career. If something didn't give, I was going to find myself in the unemployment line. I thought about my business. The future of our division was at risk, and I felt all alone now in steering this $500 million ship through the choppy seas.

I thought about my family. I'd been depriving them of quality time. I'd been moody and sullen. Instead of seeing me at my best, they'd been getting my worst.

I thought about my team. They believed I treated them as things to be used and didn't really care about them.

Suddenly, everything in my life seemed to be upside down. What had I done to deserve this? Why was this happening to me? What was going to happen next? What could I do to fix my life? Why did everything seem so tangled?

As I continued to huff, puff, and stumble down the mountain, lost in my own personal pity party, I heard the familiar whine of a two-cycle engine—a snowmobile that sounded like it was heading my way. A smiling, tanned ski patroller pulled alongside of me. "Didn't you know you're supposed to ski down the mountain?" he cracked. "This isn't a hiking trail." He laughed at his own joke, and I threw him a sarcastic smile. Maybe my expression made an impact, because he lost his grin quickly.

"Come on," he said, nodding to the seat behind him. "Jump on the back, and I'll give you a lift to the Riva Bahn chair. You can catch that and take it down to Vail Village."

As cocky as he was, I appreciated his gesture, and felt the muscles in my legs begin to unclench as we drove down the mountain. The lift operator was gracious enough to stop the chair lift so I could climb on. It was embarrassing, but far less exhausting than walking down to the bottom of the mountain, which probably would have taken a couple of hours and left me totally fatigued.

On solid ground, I worked my way back to Charter Sports to get new skis. When I arrived at the shop, the young lady who assisted me the day before recognized me. "Hi, Mr. Stevens," she said, smiling. "Need some help?"

"Uh, yeah," I said. I didn't want to sound like a total loser, so I lied about the missing ski. "I broke a ski way up on the mountain, and I need a replacement pair."

"Sure, no problem. All of our rentals are under warranty. We'll just need the broken ski. We can salvage the binding and get a replacement ski for you right away. Get you back up on the slopes in no time."

I stuttered and stammered and told her that I didn't have the ski. "I, uh, left it high on the mountain because it snapped into two pieces." *What a bogus lie*, I thought. Her look told me she wasn't buying my story. But she gave me an understanding smile and told me she'd have to charge me for the replacement skis and bindings. She took my American Express card, and fifteen minutes and $749.86 later, I was back in business with new skis. Now it wasn't just an embarrassing morning, but an expensive one, too.

I walked the short distance to Lion's Pub in Lionshead and ordered lunch. What a morning! I was tired, embarrassed, and more than a little overwhelmed with recent events. I considered returning to the hotel for a nap and skipping my ski lesson. *No*, I thought, *that wouldn't be fair to the ski instructor, bailing on him. I've got to suck it up and ski through the day.* As tough as it would be to focus, I owed it to Nancy to at least try.

I also owed it to myself.

As I reflected on the morning, the thoughts about my career, business, and family stayed with me. It just wasn't working. None of it. I realized something had to give. I wasn't sure what to do, but there were a number of things that weren't turning out the way I'd planned. My life was in need of a serious overhaul.

I've got this week to get some things in order, I told myself as I stared out the window at the crowds of people walking by. *This week I've got to come up with a plan.*

CHAPTER THIRTEEN

Meeting Ed

That afternoon I stood under the Lionshead clock tower and searched the crowd for the famous one-piece blue ski suits with silver and black stripes that Vail ski instructors wear. At precisely 1:30 p.m., a smiling man in his early sixties with a name tag that read "Ed, Darien, Connecticut" walked up to me.

"Ben Stevens?"

He was silver-haired and tanned, with a nice smile. He was healthy looking, in better shape than I was, the kind of distinguished looking gentleman you would see skippering a fifty-foot sailboat in a financial products ad. He exuded a relaxed, confident air. I nodded and stuck out my hand. "You must be Ed."

My first thought was that he was much older than I thought he would be. I was a bit disappointed that Ed wasn't younger, and I wondered if ski lessons with this old guy were going to be a drag.

My eyes lit up. His advanced age was going to give me the out I so desperately wanted. If the day turned out to be a bust, I could tell him I had a change in plans and wouldn't need his help the rest of the week. And I wouldn't feel too badly about it. It would be like renting a yacht, and then realizing it was only a battered old rowboat. Nobody, not even Nancy, would blame me for cutting it short. After all, I wouldn't want the old guy to break a hip. I felt a wave of relief wash over me. I was going to get back to work early after all.

After our introduction, I shared with Ed the high recommendations he received from our friends the Morems. "Boy, they couldn't stop talking about you," I said, forcing a smile. "'You want an instructor,' they said, "'Ed's your man.'" As the words left my mouth, they sounded disingenuous, a bit lame, like I was sucking up to him. It struck me as odd, particularly since I don't usually worry about how genuine or false I sound. What was it about this guy that made me feel guilty for treating him like a geriatric patient?

If he noticed I was putting on a fake smile, he didn't show it. "Thanks," he said. "That's nice to hear. I really love what I do. My ski clients are all either repeat customers or their referrals." Ed was gracious and warm, and it struck me how strong his eye contact was. There was something about him that immediately let you know he was really listening to you, not thinking about the next thing he was going to say. I wasn't sure exactly what it was, but something about Ed made an immediate impact on me. The guy grabbed my attention.

While I was still lukewarm to the ski lessons, I reworked my first impression of Ed. He seemed like he might be okay. Perhaps I shouldn't have instantly written him off.

Ed started asking questions. He wasn't pushy; he seemed genuinely interested. "Where are you from? How frequently do you ski? When did you ski last? What level of skier are you? What do I need to do to make sure you have a great ski vacation at Vail?" He had probably asked these questions hundreds of times to his clients, but he listened closely to my every word. It was clear he quickly builds close bonds with others. He looked at the clock tower. "What do you say we start skiing?"

"Sounds good to me," I said, and we hopped on the Eagle Bahn gondola. On our way up, I started asking Ed about himself. "Well," he said. "I'm retired. My wife and I live in Connecticut."

"Been doing this long?"

"Almost fifteen years. Even when I worked full-time, I was a part-time instructor at Okemo Mountain in southern Vermont. Now I come to Vail January through March every season to ski and teach."

"Skiing every day," I said, watching the gorgeous scenery outside the gondola. "Sounds like about the best retirement I can imagine."

"I love people and helping them with skiing and other areas of their lives. I sit on a couple of nonprofit boards, but what I really love is getting to know people and helping them, however I can. My intention is to be a contribution to other people. It's the reason I'm here."

"Your wife doesn't mind you coming out here for three months every year?"

"Nah. Three years ago, she and I bought a condo in West Vail. Sally comes out here for a few weeks at a time during the winter, but she really loves to stick around Connecticut. Kids and grandchildren, you know."

I nodded and thought of my own kids. I wondered what they were up to. "How many?"

He smiled and pulled out his wallet. "Thought you'd never ask. Three children and six grandchildren." He walked me through each of their photos, telling me a little bit about each kid. "And this is Sally," he said proudly, pointing to a picture of a beautiful woman in her early sixties surrounded by all of her grandchildren. "She'll be coming into town this weekend."

He obviously loved his new career and family and seemed extremely happy. As the gondola slowed, I realized that the man sitting next to me had everything I ever wanted.

We skied a few runs. Ed had me working on parallel turns in the light powder. He encouraged me to work on banking and down-flexion, together with counter-rotation. "This is the best initiation for parallel turning in the new snow," he said, and I believed him. I could feel the difference as my turns became crisper and crisper. My confidence level was surging. My disastrous morning was beginning to fade away.

The afternoon flew by quickly. Then, at about 2:45 p.m., on what would be the last chair lift ride up the mountain for the day, my cell phone rang in the pocket of my ski parka. The caller ID showed that it was Dan Arrington's cell phone.

"I need to take this, Ed," I said. "Excuse me."

"Absolutely." Ed smiled and turned away, to give me as much privacy as he could.

I opened my phone. "Dan," I said curtly. "What's your plan?" As Dan spoke, my face stiffened. I listened as he explained that he met with the president of Softwrite. The situation for them was worse than we thought.

"Seventy percent of Softwrite's business has been with one technology firm that's now in bankruptcy," Dan said, his voice even less confident than it was when we spoke the night before. "That's left Softwrite holding the bag with a huge accounts receivable on the books and a serious shortage of working capital."

I thought about throwing the phone from the chair lift. "What about your guys? Have they found another company that could help us fix the software?"

"We found another company, but they can't help us for at least sixty days, too late for our upcoming launch."

"You're telling me another firm isn't a viable option."

"Right."

I felt a rush of blood run to my head, frustration enveloping me. I barked at Dan. "Their problem has now become our problem. We wouldn't be in this predicament if you knew what you were doing. Dan, I don't think you can find your butt with both hands!"

I knew I'd raised my voice, but I didn't know how loud I was until the couple in the chair lift in front of us turned around to look at me. Ed had turned back toward me and was listening to every word. The expression on his weathered face was tough to read, but I swore I saw a glimmer in his eyes.

I didn't care if he heard me yelling at Dan. I didn't care if the whole mountain heard me. "You tell this guy that he's got to fix this problem for us, or we'll tie them up in lawsuits so fast it'll make his head spin."

I let loose a string of profanities into the cell phone. "You call Jean and tell her I said to hire a California law firm to get on them immediately! Whatever we have to do to fix this problem. Fast! Am I clear, Dan?"

"Yes."

"Dan, let me tell you, this is serious. This must be fixed—immediately. My patience on this matter–and with you–is almost at its end. Have I made myself clear?"

I heard nothing in return for what seemed like an eternity and I asked again, "Dan, did you hear me? Are you there?"

Dan replied weakly. "Yes."

"Good. Now get going. Talk to Jean, then go back to Softwrite. Get tough with them. Call me tomorrow with an update."

After the call, there was an uncomfortable silence on the chair lift. It felt like my harsh words were echoing through the valleys below our feet.

I glanced at Ed. He looked at me and shook his head. "Tough call."

"Yeah," I said, unconvinced that Ed had ever had to make a call nearly that difficult. He wouldn't get it, I figured, and my voice took on a patronizing sheen. "Comes with the territory, I guess. One of my guys really screwed up, and it may cause us to blow the year. This is a really bad situation."

Ed nodded, and we disembarked from the chair in silence. I began tightening my boots and making my other pre-run adjustments, but my hands were shaking from the adrenaline rushing through my body.

Ed knelt next to me as I struggled to buckle my boots. His voice was warm, and somehow managed to soften the sharp spikes pounding in my head. "Listening to you seemed like déjà vu to me. Reminded me of how I used to act twenty years ago."

I nodded and concentrated on getting my boots buckled. *However he acted twenty years ago, it wasn't anything like that,* I thought. *What was the worst he had to deal with back then? A broken Model T?* He didn't understand what it was like for me. He never could.

Then, far more quickly than I thought he could move, he leaped to his feet. "Listen, what do you say we call it a day? You've got a lot on your mind." He patted me on the shoulder, and laughed, as if he hadn't a care in the world. "We're on tomorrow morning. Meet you at 9:00 a.m. at the Lionshead clock tower. I'm out of here. Nice to meet you."

With that, Ed skied off. *I must have sounded like a real jerk on that call,* I thought. Ed couldn't wait to escape. As I continued to ponder Ed's hasty departure, I began to feel my face begin to redden again. After all, Ed was working for me. I was paying his salary. That abrupt exit was rude. And that déjà vu business? He didn't even know me and he compared me to how he used to be?

Oh, I suppose he's better than me now, I thought. *And furthermore, what does he know about my business? My career is about to go in the tank if we can't get the software problem fixed. I'm going to have to fire Dan, and my ski instructor laughs at me and abruptly leaves? What gives?*

I got my boots buckled, and skied down Bwana. By the time I made it the bottom, I was exhausted, both physically and mentally. I was frustrated. I was angry. I decided to go back to the hotel and take a nap.

As I tossed and turned, one thought rolled through my head: Just who the hell did Ed Davis think he was?

CHAPTER FOURTEEN

Waiting out the Fog

When I awoke, the clock on my bedside table showed 6:26 a.m. I rolled around and tried to fall back asleep for an hour, but to no avail. I had actually slept ten hours, which was odd since I typically sleep six hours or less. *When was the last time I slept that long?* I thought. *When I was twenty-one?*

Thoughts kept racing through my mind. The tangled emotions about what was going on at work. My wipeout. I thought about Dan and the software problem, but I kept coming back to how I made an ass of myself in front of my ski instructor, when he heard me berate Dan on the phone.

My entire body felt like it had been pounded with a meat tenderizer. I was sore all over and very stiff. My back hurt, my shins, thighs, and ankles ached. I was sure some of it was from the skiing, but I guessed that more was from the wipeout and my humiliating march down the mountain.

I grabbed the remote, turned on the TV and surfed to Channel 8, where *Good Morning Vail* was on. A perky weather man chirped the forecast. A warm front had moved in and the day's high was going to be in the high forties at the base of the mountain and low forties at the mountaintop. "As the warm air hits the snow pack, I expect fog in the morning," he said. "But it'll likely lift by noon."

I dragged my body to the window and opened the curtains. It was so foggy, I could barely see the mountain.

It'll burn off before we hit the slopes, I told myself, and eased into a hot shower. I got myself ready for the day, moving slowly because of the dull pain shooting through my entire body. I grabbed a bagel and coffee in the lobby, and then headed out the door to the mountain. A check of the outside thermometer at Charter Sports' ski corral where they kept my skis and poles at night showed forty degrees at 8:30 a.m. At 8:45, I saw Ed walking up to me at the Lionshead clock tower—without his ski equipment.

"Good morning, Ben. I hear the start is going to be delayed this morning until the fog lifts." He didn't mention my outburst yesterday, and I decided not to bring it up either. We made small talk for a bit, and he told me he guessed the lifts would open at 10:00 or 10:30 a.m., plenty of time to get in a full day of skiing.

"You like coffee?" he asked, nodding toward the main strip, now bustling with people who'd been expecting to ski and seemed to be walking aimlessly from shop to shop. "What do you say we grab a cup and wait out this soupy fog?"

We took the short walk to McCarthy's. I placed the order for us while Ed secured two bar stools at the counter, near the server. Ed had a large cup of black coffee, and I ordered a double espresso.

He took a sip. "So, how was your night?"

"Uneventful," I said. "I've got a lot going on at work and was pretty focused on that." I glanced at the ground. "Mostly the problem you overheard yesterday on the phone."

"I'm glad you brought up the phone call. Hope you didn't take my response and comments yesterday the wrong way. You see, as I overheard your discussion, it really did remind me of my past. I used to react that way when I received bad news, too."

Not wanting to re-hash yesterday's call with Ed, and hoping he would drop the topic, I replied in a biting tone.

"Ed, with all due respect, you overheard a portion of a discussion with someone on my team who has operated incompetently and managed to put our company's immediate future at significant risk. I don't think you fully understand the circumstances at play here, and I wonder if maybe you're stepping into territory beyond ski instruction."

Ed smiled. "You're absolutely right. I'm sure I don't understand the circumstances, and it really doesn't have anything to do with our skiing." He looked me directly in the eye. "But I understand enough about human behavior to know some things. Listening to you and the harsh way you spoke to that person, you really reminded me of the way I used to be."

I was beginning to get annoyed with this old dude. He just didn't get it. Why the hell didn't that fog hurry up and burn off so we could stop talking and get back to the slopes? "Okay, okay. I was a bit rough with him, and I'm sorry you had to hear that. And I'll bite. You keep mentioning that I reminded you of the way you were twenty-plus years ago. How so?" I asked, hoping his explanation would solve his need to belabor the issue.

He took another sip of coffee. "Ben, may I tell you a short story—about the 'Old Ed'?"

"Sure, fire away," I half-heartedly replied, knowing we had nothing but time as we waited for the fog to clear and the chair lifts to run. And one way or another, he had a point to make and wasn't going to let this thing drop until he made it with me. I squirmed on my stool.

"When I was forty-three, I was named president of a prestigious public relations firm in New York City. The firm had been around for about sixty years at the time; you'd certainly recognize its name. It was my first general management role." He smiled and his eyes crinkled, as if he was replaying some fond memories in his head. "I had been a hard charger and successful at business development, but in retrospect, I was absolutely unprepared to lead others and to be entrusted as the steward of the firm's future.

"I had focused my energy on bringing in new business, and had gotten things accomplished through my own push. I was very much ego-driven. You know, a go-go guy, justifying my actions in the name of execution, always doing. Someone who was identified by his accomplishments and the trappings of success. You know the type."

Yeah, I thought. *I knew the type.*

"In what could only be described as an act of total arrogance, I mistakenly thought I'd make my mark and impress the board and shareholders by setting a goal to increase revenues by 20 percent in the first year. The people reporting to me thought I was crazy. But at the time, I honestly believed I was so special and talented, I could will the firm to increase business this dramatically, just based on my own belief in my ability to execute. No new services or products, no acquisitions, no new nothing—just by having superstar Ed at the helm. I didn't fully understand the firm's history or know much about its people. And, to be honest with you, I really didn't care."

As I listened to Ed talk, I realized he knew more about what I was going through than I thought. A lot more.

"In less than two years, my directive and pacesetting style of operating, and the pressure I created, caused the three best executives under me to leave. They started their own firm and took with them several of our largest accounts. And then things got even worse. There was no buy-in to the recovery plan I implemented. By that time, I had totally alienated the rest of the people at the firm. I had created such a toxic climate, particularly for my direct reports, not a single person stood in my corner when things got really choppy."

"So what happened?" I asked, now more interested in Ed's story.

He smiled. "The chairman fired me. I was out of work for the first time in my career. It was devastating. It took me about a year and a half to find a new job. And that was a time before executives were frequently fired, like you see today."

"Man," I said. "Tough break."

"Those eighteen months were both the most painful and the most enlightening period in my professional life. Painful because my ego was severely bruised. I was viewed as damaged goods, and I seriously doubted whether I deserved, much less would get, another leadership position within the PR industry." He sipped at his coffee. "But it was also enlightening, because I had the time to reflect and learn from my experiences. During this time I had the good fortune to meet a gentleman by the name of David Carvelli, who proved to be a teacher, coach, and mentor for me. He taught me some valuable lessons that I reflected on and learned. Fortunately, I listened and applied what David taught me, and my life dramatically changed for the better."

"How?" I said, leaning forward. "How did it change for the better?" I realized that he'd hooked me like a mackerel on a jig. I felt my face begin to warm. The story was hitting so close to home, I needed him to keep talking.

"David was the founder of a networking group that is still based in Stamford—a group whose purpose was to connect out-of-work executives so they could trade job leads and keep one another motivated. In fact, I still stop by their meetings once a month or so when I'm back in Connecticut to see if I can help anyone out. Well, David was a retired executive who made his fortune running an international trading company. He was a wise man who came into my life at a time when I needed his wisdom. He died five years ago."

Ed's eyes began to mist a bit, but he kept talking. "David taught me that every moment we're awake, we have an initial choice to make. We have a choice about our way of being toward others. What drives our way of being? It's really driven by one of the two basic human motivations—fear or love. This choice business even precedes behavior. We make our choice every waking moment of every day in every human interaction. It's as simple as that. I didn't appreciate this earlier in my life, but learned it from David in my mid-forties. And I've been trying to apply this principle ever since. The knowledge David shared with me helped me re-think things and plan my career and life in a more fulfilling direction."

This is the fuzziest concept I've ever heard, I thought. "You had me, but then you lost me. You need to explain this to me. I don't think I get it."

"I'm not surprised you don't get it," Ed said, his eyes crinkling again. "I didn't get it at first either. Let me explain to you how it works."

And he drew me in again.

"When we're motivated by fear, we are blind to the reality of others. When we're motivated by fear, which I believe too many people are too much of the time, our focus is on ourselves. In this state of fear, we are driven by our ego. Our focus is self-centered. It's characterized by negativity and limitations. All negativity stems from fear, and you know what they say fear is: False Evidence Appearing Real. When we are motivated by fear, we experience a mindset that can be described by negativity, blame, guilt, pessimism, anxiety, anger, and fear itself. We often see life as a zero-sum game— for me to win, someone else must lose."

That was exactly how I saw things. Me against them. Even in my personal life, it was never all of us together, on the same side. Too often, it was competition and conflict.

"When we are enlightened, on the other hand, we are motivated by love." I cringed. Ed didn't seem ashamed or afraid to use the term "love." But some guys, including myself, are a little embarrassed to use that word.

"Trust me, there is nothing unmanly about what I'm going to share with you," Ed said. "When we are motivated by love, we see ourselves and others as genuine people with real aspirations, dreams, cares, and feelings. We don't let our egos drive us in this state. Instead, we are driven by something deeper—something that's within all of us. So, do we focus on negative emotions, judgment, cynicism, and unforgiving thoughts and actions, or do we focus on something that is the opposite of fear for ourselves and others?"

He paused for a moment to let the words sink in. "The opposite of fear is love. Love and fear and light and darkness are a lot alike. For instance, darkness isn't a thing—it's an absence of light. When we turn on a light, the darkness disappears. David taught me that if we lead with love, fear recedes and ultimately disappears. Most people have a tendency to fight against fear, but the real opportunity is not to fight fear, but to turn up the dial on love."

He looked at me through squinty eyes, as if he was trying to get a read on my reaction. "Now, I know you're probably thinking this sounds very soft. But it's really about as soft as a brick once you understand and apply some basic concepts. May I continue to explain?"

I nodded, my interest genuinely rising.

"First of all, I think you can tell the love I'm describing isn't romantic love. This type of love is about positive intentions, vision, abundance, harmony, hope, and forgiveness. When we focus on these qualities, when we work together, all sorts of possibilities open up for ourselves and others. It's about respect, genuine concern, and good feeling toward others. And the best way we can show love toward others–and ourselves–is by making another important choice.

"When we lead with love, we see others as people, with concerns, feelings, hopes, and dreams. When we lead with fear, we see others as things, not as people—things to be used or ignored."

He sipped at his coffee. "Deep down, our soul knows what is right, but we have to tune in. And once we tune in, we can see what's right—and that's to treat individuals as people. That's the way we want to be treated, isn't it? We can be responsive to this feeling and treat people the way we want to be treated. Or we can choose not to be responsive. It is our choice."

He raised an eyebrow. It was a subtle change in his expression, but I knew he was referring to me. "We can disregard this feeling. If we ignore our feeling to do what is right toward another, we'll think of all kinds of reasons to convince ourselves that we are right and the other person wrong. This is our ego speaking, by the way, and not our soul.

"But when we're motivated by love and see others genuinely as people, we can take an important step in loosening the grip our own ego has on us. We lessen our own self-importance, we stop being offended by others, we let go of our need to be right and to always win, we let go of identifying ourselves on the basis of our achievements."

He nodded toward the bar. "For example, I couldn't help but notice how you ordered our coffee from the woman at the counter. Did you see her as a person or a thing?"

"Hey, I just ordered our coffee, nothing more or less. I was fine with her." As I spoke, I realized that it sounded like I was trying to defend my behavior.

"Ben, my new friend," Ed said, "I've got news for you. I saw the interaction. I think if you asked *her* whether you saw her as a person or a thing, she wouldn't say person. What do you think?"

"Maybe," I said. "I guess there's always room for improvement." Deep down, I knew Ed was right. I hated being corrected, but as he pointed out my interaction with the waitress, he did so in a supportive, kind way that softened the blow. Sort of how a skilled coach might.

"We can be enlightened or we can be in the dark," he continued. "There is no middle ground. Love or fear. People or things. Supportive or not. There is no in-between. You make the choices before you say anything—and I dare say these choices are the most important ones you make in your life."

Ed was shooting straight with me. The way he did it made me realize he was truly interested in helping me see the light, not just correcting my behavior. Still, my stomach was beginning to tie itself in knots.

"Let's go back to the call I overheard yesterday," he said. "What was the name of the guy who called you?"

Oh no, I thought, *we can't seem to get away from that call.* "Dan," I answered sheepishly.

"Okay, now suppose we asked Dan how he felt about the call. What do you think he'd say?"

A flicker of anger over Dan's incompetence momentarily covered up my regret over acting like a jerk. "He'd probably say I'm a demanding SOB, but that he screwed up, too, if he's honest. He'd also say he's got a tough problem he's got to fix or our business faces dire consequences." I felt my mouth tighten as I spoke. "He's got a performance problem, and he needs to deal with that."

"Fine," Ed said. "We'll assume there is a problem with Dan's performance. So if we asked Dan if he feels he's been treated as a person by you, what do you think he would say? Did he feel love from you, or fear? Were you receptive to and supportive of his needs, or not?"

I thought about it. As angry as I was about the news Dan delivered, Ed was right. I had verbally bludgeoned Dan, with no regard for how he was feeling. "He would say he felt fear, I believe," I said softly. "He would also say I was not tuned into his needs."

Ed nodded. "Do you think this approach will motivate Dan to fix his performance shortfalls?"

"It might if he wants to stay employed."

"Ben, I think you know better than that. I learned the hard way–this is firsthand experience talking–that while fear may change behaviors in the short term, it will never, ever win hearts, and will thus always fail in the long run."

"It makes sense," I conceded. "I know when someone has put the screws to me, it makes me want to succeed in spite of them, not because of them."

"Exactly!" He glanced out the window. "One last question for you. You've been insistent that Dan has problems performing. Could it be that you have contributed to Dan's problem?"

It was difficult to answer. "Yeah, I guess I haven't helped Dan as I could have. I've probably added to the problem."

Ed quickly shifted gears. "What my mentor David showed me is there are two ways to do almost anything. Let's take an example. We can give compliments or we can give constructive feedback. And we can give the compliments or feedback in a supportive or resistant way. Get it?"

"Keep talking."

"Let's say you have a difference of opinion with your wife on an issue one morning before you leave the house for work. You and she go back and forth on the issue, trying to convince the other to see the merits of your position. You continue this discussion until it turns into an argument. You've now been at it for ten minutes. You look at your watch and decide if you don't leave the house now, you'll be late for the Monday morning operations review. At the moment, that's a less desirable happening than this discussion with your wife. You don't want to be late for that important meeting, so you go up to your wife, tell her she has beautiful eyes and that you love her. You give her a hug and a quick kiss. Then out the door you go.

"When giving this compliment, would you say you were motivated by fear or love, did you see her as a person or thing, were you supportive of her needs? And, by the way, how did you think your wife would respond to such a compliment?"

"I think we both know the answer. Not very favorably, I'm afraid," I replied.

"Exactly right, Ben. You're getting it. Now back to Dan. It's not that we let up on the performance issue, but it's about how we address it with the person that makes the difference. What I learned is if we need to be hard at work on expectations and performance and we wish to be effective, we have no choice but to be receptive to and supportive of the needs of others and treat them as people."

The sun was beginning to shine into the window, but I barely noticed.

"Now, if we fail to do what we sense is right in dealing with another, we create a problem for ourselves," Ed said. "Our ego goes into overdrive and leads us into a monologue of why we are correct in doing something we know isn't *really* right. If we're not careful, our ego leads us down a continuous rationalization spiral. We rationalize and rationalize our position to prove to ourselves that we're right and others are wrong, and we do this to our own detriment. We become wrapped up into our selves and feel self-important. When we're self-important, we are easily offended by something or someone. We may develop an insatiable desire to win, be right, and seen as superior. And down the spiral we go. Our ego takes us on an out-of-control trip."

My mind flashed on my own recent out-of-control trip, the one where I crashed down the mountainside.

"Now, I'm not saying you are or aren't going down this downward spiral. Only you know. But I can tell you from first-hand experience, it's one I went down in 1985 and for many years before.

"When David first shared these concepts with me–love, treating people as people, being supportive–to be honest with you, even after my disastrous performance as president of that company, my ego wouldn't let me fully acknowledge that I was the one with the problem. Isn't that wild? But I soon learned *I* was the problem, and not anyone else. And as soon as I realized that fact, I was ready for a breakthrough."

"How did you figure out you were the problem?" I asked.

"David introduced me to a diagram he called the 'relationship wheel.' As I pondered this diagram and thought deeply about the state of my relationships, it was an undeniable truth that I was, indeed, the one with the problem. So it was that day, November 4, 1985, to be exact, that I committed to change the way I operate. I swore I'd do my best to be motivated by love, to see others as people, and be receptive to what I believed was right. And, thank God I did. If I hadn't, I'm not sure where I'd be today."

"Can you share the–what did you call it–relationship wheel with me?"

Ed smiled and pulled a pen out of his pocket, grabbed a napkin that was under his coffee cup, and drew a large circle on the napkin. Next to it, he wrote, "On a scale of one (low) to ten (high), how would you honestly score the state of your relationships?" He divided the circle like a pie and wrote a different word on each piece: Friends, Significant Others, Children, Parents and Siblings, Boss, Direct Reports, Peers, and Others.

As I read the diagram Ed constructed for me, he must have seen me wince. Mercifully, he didn't ask me the question I dreaded: "Ben, how would you score on each of the spokes?"

Instead, he folded up the napkin and gave it to me, saying, "It might be useful to keep this and refer to it time to time."

Ed glanced at his watch. "It's almost 10:30. We've been talking for ninety minutes. What do you say we see if the fog has cleared?" The restaurant was nearly empty, and sun was shining through the windows. I blinked against the sunlight and smiled.

We walked together in silence to the gondola station and saw the lifts moving and skiers getting aboard. Ed headed toward the ski instructors' offices to retrieve his equipment and said he'd meet me in a half an hour at the Eagle Bahn gondola.

As I watched Ed walk away, I reflected on our discussion, pulling the napkin from my pocket and staring at the relationship wheel he had drawn. Rate my satisfaction with each key relationship in my life on a scale of one to ten, he had said, so I did. I quickly jotted a number onto each of the pie pieces, and was instantly struck by how low they were. Two for direct reports. Four for peers. Three for my boss. I hadn't scored a single one over six, not even my relationships with Nancy or the kids. I'd never thought about it that way before, and I felt a pang of regret in my gut. Why didn't I consider relationships more important? Wasn't I supposed to have some people in my life I felt more connected to? I stared at the numbers. They were so low and told a revealing story.

Was it my friends' and family's fault our relationships were so weak? My mind flashed back to the day before, when I tumbled helplessly down the mountain. From the way my back and legs ached, it was obvious that I didn't know as much as I thought I did about skiing. I was painfully aware that even though I assumed I knew what I was doing, I wasn't always making the best decisions. *Maybe I was to blame for the state of my relationships*, I thought. *Maybe it's me.*

I had to find a way to improve the relationships. Something had to change.

I may have found the seeds of my recovery plan this morning, I thought.

I took a deep breath, grabbed my cell phone, and dialed Dan's number. It rang a few times, then rolled into voicemail.

"Look, Dan," I said. "I just wanted you to know that we're in this situation together, and we're going to figure out a way to get out of this mess. I know you're feeling a lot of personal responsibility and stress, and my actions the past few days no doubt were contributing more to the problem than toward a solution." I paused. "That's it. Why don't you call me tonight, and we can talk about it more."

Then I called Nancy. I got her voicemail, as well. "Hi, babe. Just checking in. Things are good. Yeah, that's right. They're good. I'll explain more later. I decided not to come home early. I've been doing a lot of thinking here, rolling some ideas around. And I think I can make a little more progress before I leave. And, honey, thanks for hooking me up with Ed."

As I finished up the messages, I took a few deep breaths of the clear mountain air and saw the sun was shining brightly through the clouds. As the fog lifted and the sun began to pour over the mountain, it looked like we had a beautiful day ahead of us.

I'm not sure if it was my talk with Ed, the sun, or a combination of both, but I was definitely feeling better, more hopeful. I grabbed my MP3 player, found Ziggy Marley and the Melody Makers' *Live-Volume 1* CD, and played–what else?–*Beautiful Day.*

It was time to hit the slopes.

• • •

Ed suggested we take the Wildwood express chair lift to access some of the steepest runs on Vail Mountain. Although I was a little hesitant to repeat my wipeout from the day before, I agreed to give it a shot.

Ed insisted the only way to improve my skiing ability was to attempt more challenging terrain. "Skiing steep slopes tests your nerve and your ability to control your turns," Ed said, smiling. "Don't worry. You've got it in you. And I'll be right beside you the whole way down."

We skied Deuces Wild, Wild Card, and Kangaroo Cornice, plus several other runs. Ed explained that the key to turning on steep slopes was to keep the radius of my turns short—in other words, to get around quickly. "You've gotta be nimble," he said as he demonstrated the turns. "You need to be able to use your edges effectively to check your speed—either by carving a tight turn from one traverse to the next, or by preparing for each turn with a sharp 'edge set.'"

Ed led, I followed, and I was pleasantly surprised by how well I skied on the extremely steep slopes. He took us on some terrain that really pushed me, and his ski instruction made a big difference in my being able to navigate and have fun on the very challenging runs. Following my tumble down the mountain on Monday, I would have never tried the steeps without Ed's encouragement. But there I was, gliding effortlessly down the beautiful mountain. After a while, my wipeout was nothing more than a painful memory, and I concentrated on enjoying myself. I thought about the spry, almost sixty-five-year-old instructor skiing next to me, and I realized that Ed's instruction and advice had become just as important pieces of equipment as my skis and poles.

Ed and I skied together until about noon, and I have to confess I was sorry to see him go when he departed for his 1:00 p.m. lesson. We agreed to hook up the next day at mid-Vail for lunch and our next lesson.

As I grabbed a bite at the Road House, at the peak of the mountain near the Mountaintop Express chair lift, I reflected on what was a breakthrough day. Ed had given me valuable tips on skiing the steeps. But even more valuable, by sharing his experience at the PR firm, his crash, and what he learned, he gave me some meaningful insights into my own life. The muscles in my legs ached from gripping the steeps, and my mind was churning with the nuggets Ed had imparted.

I spent the rest of the day strolling around Vail, then reading quietly in my room. For dinner, I went to Fiesta's, which had been voted the "Best of Vail" in the Mexican restaurant category. The chimichanga was fantastic, and I found myself sitting there for hours, just listening to the mariachi band and thinking about what a lucky guy I was.

I returned to the hotel, and checked my email and voice-mail to see if there were any updates from Dan. Nothing. I decided to soak in the outdoor Jacuzzi and called it a night.

CHAPTER FIFTEEN

Creating Executive Value Lessons

I woke up refreshed and revitalized. Waiting for me in my email inbox was a message from Dan. He thanked me for the voicemail I left and asked if we could connect at 6:00 p.m. Minnesota time for a conference call with Jean, our in-house attorney, to further discuss the software situation. His message was a bit cryptic, and I was intrigued. He suggested there might be an out-of-the-box solution that was a potential breakthrough to our problem, and he was looking forward to discussing it with me on our call.

I felt a tiny bit of encouragement trickle through my body. I was dying to call Dan to find out what he meant, but I withheld the urge and replied that I'd call in at 6:00 p.m. to hear the details.

I stretched out on the bed and let it all sink in. As I reflected on the events of the day before, it became more and more apparent that Ed had helped me become aware of a problem I simply didn't recognize I had. I had been deceiving myself and justifying my behavior.

The challenge was now how to figure out a solution to my problem. The choices Ed laid out for me were valid. I listened to his words echo in my head. Every day we have a choice to be motivated by love or fear, to see others as people or things, and to be responsive to what we feel is right or not. "We make our choice every waking moment of every day in every human interaction," Ed had said. "It's as simple as that."

It made all the sense in the world. These choices, I had to admit, were pretty basic. Had I been interacting with others in my life according to these choices? Certainly not consistently, and particularly not in the past few years. Why? I guess the honest answer was that it had to do with my drive, my desire to get results, my need to appear right and in control. In other words, my ego. The more I thought about it, the more I began to feel some twinges of guilt—for how I'd treated the individuals on my team, for the way I'd treated my family.

I considered the feedback I received from the 360-degree assessment. I felt guilty that I hadn't done more to connect with others. I'd known that some of the members of my team saw me as a tyrant—and now I had the undeniable data to support it. I remembered some of the comments I received and winced at the severity of the language my team had used:

- "Ben has not proven he is able to effectively bring an executive team together."
- "Ben uses people to gain results; he doesn't really see us as people, but more like things or tools."
- "The hub-and-spoke management style isn't conducive to real teamwork."
- "He's the Lone Ranger."
- "With Ben, you are guilty until proven innocent."
- "Ben's dominant leadership styles are directive and turning up the pace. No motivation, no coaching, no meaningful participation."

What's the best way, I wondered, *to make the changes that are obviously required? How can I apply these concepts in working with the team? How do I apply them to each individual on the team? Is my ego out of control?* If my direct reports weren't getting what they needed from me, it seemed that maybe I must be the one who needed to change. But how? The more I pondered the situation the more frustrating it became.

I began to wonder what Nancy and the kids would say about me if they were asked to provide their assessment, then brushed the thought away. I wasn't sure I wanted to know the answer.

I was now as confused as I was the day before, when Ed and I first spoke. *I've got to talk with Ed about this*, I told myself. This would be the first topic for our meeting later in the day. The skiing instruction could wait. This was far more important.

I decided to get in a workout at the fitness center in the hotel, and I didn't get to the mountain until 11:00 a.m. I skied the Lionshead side of the mountain for an hour before heading to mid-Vail to meet with Ed.

At exactly 12:30 p.m., I saw Ed making his way through the lodge at mid-Vail. He was an easy guy to spot—tall and distinguished, with silver hair and that unmistakable blue ski instructor suit with silver and black stripes. We saw one another, exchanged greetings, and decided to get some lunch outside at the burger stand. We got our food and plopped down into a couple of recliners to bask in the warm Colorado sun. I was so anxious to pick his brain, I quickly forgot all about my hamburger.

"Listen, Ed," I said. "Thanks again for an excellent day yesterday. The skiing was the best—thanks for that. I've been thinking a lot about what we discussed."

"Good for you," Ed said, setting his burger on the chair in front of him and giving me his undivided attention.

"I can't stop thinking about it all. I can see that I have choices to make. My challenge is how to apply them. How did you make these choices real day in and day out at work? Didn't people see you as soft? Weren't you taken advantage of?" I felt my voice speeding up, like an excited child. "How did you get people to do what needed to be done, and still be true to the choices? These are the questions that I'm wrestling with."

"Ah," Ed said. "So the big question you're asking is how do we apply the knowledge on a day-to-day basis? How do we apply it in a more practical way? Is that what you're wondering?"

"Exactly," I said. "That's where I'm stuck."

Ed leaned forward slightly. "I mentioned my mentor David Carvelli. Well, David gave me some valuable insights as to how to bring this knowledge into everyday life as a leader of others. And if I do say so myself, I've learned a few things, too, in the executive roles I held following the transition to the 'new Ed.'"

"That's exactly where I'm struggling," I confessed.

"Well, the leader's job is to get results, right? A leader decides what must be done. No results, no need for a leader. But how the leader gets results is key. David taught me there is an important cause-and-effect chain that each leader sets off, for better or worse. You can think about connecting the dots to see how this chain works. He told me the best leaders—you know, the real 'A' players, the top 10 percent—are ones who operate very differently from their lower-performing colleagues. Do you know the major characteristic that separates the A players from the B and C players?"

"Let's see. Probably their drive, work ethic, and their sheer intelligence. Their IQ," I replied.

Ed smiled. "I hate to be the bearer of bad news here, but you're 180 degrees off on this one."

"Come on," I said, a little bit of annoyance creeping into my voice. "I can't be that far off."

"There have been a number of studies that have explored what it is that differentiates high performing executives from their lower-performing colleagues. The results are fascinating."

I settled into my recliner.

"The results showed that IQ, technical training, and previous work or industry experience don't explain executive success. These areas aren't differentiators—they are really only threshold competencies and experiences. In other words, in order to be, let's say, a CEO of a company, you must be a reasonably smart person. That's a given. A relatively high IQ is a requirement for the job. But a higher IQ doesn't explain why one executive will be a better performer than another."

I raised my eyebrow. "That's a fact?"

"Yep. Neither does technical training, drive, or where we went to college or what kind of grades we got. In fact, these factors were found to contribute only between 4 and 25 percent of the success of these top players. So that leaves between 75 and 96 percent of the success that must be attributable to other factors." Ed paused to take a bite of food, and then asked, "Do you want to know what those factors are?"

"You better believe I do!" I said.

"Well, listen closely, Ben. The real factors that differentiate top performance in executives are four fundamental capabilities: self-awareness, self-control, empathy, and relationship skills. These four capabilities are critical to top performance. They're supported by research I alluded to, as well as my own experience."

I patted my pockets. "Should I be taking notes?"

"No need. Remembering and applying the choices I discussed with you yesterday will help you get a handle on these four capabilities. The good news is the more experience we gain, the more likely we are to develop these four capabilities. Unlike IQ, they are developable and grow with experience and age.

"In the old days when people spoke of someone who was experienced and wise, they often indirectly were referring to these capabilities. Now, they have a name. These capabilities provide the foundation for what is now called emotional intelligence. And there's more good news. If you are motivated to become more emotionally intelligent, there are steps you can take that will help you build these capabilities."

"Yeah, I've read a little about emotional intelligence," I said. "And I can see how focusing on the three choices we discussed yesterday before we act can help us with self-awareness, self-control, and our relationships. But what I still don't get is how to put this knowledge into action in a practical way, particularly with my direct reports. You can add my wife and kids to the list, too."

"Okay, okay. I'm not quite done yet. Let me show you how the dots connect." He grabbed a napkin, pulled out a pen and drew four circles, with a different phrase in each: Emotional Intelligence, Leadership Styles, Working Climate, and Results.

At the top of the page he wrote "Creating Executive Value," and under that, "Leaders create the climate for success."

"Now, I'm going to show you how the emotional intelligence gets applied in your interactions with your direct reports and others at work." He looked me in the eye. "It's how you use the leadership styles."

"Go on," I said, taking a bite out of my burger.

"You're the president of a big division of a large global medical company. And you've got a lot of complex matters that you undoubtedly wrestle with in that job."

"Damn straight," I said.

"While the situations that leaders find themselves are infinite in number, they tend to use one or a combination of six leadership styles when working with others to get results. These styles, or patterns of behavior, are not a function of your personality, but of a strategic choice you make, based on your analysis of the situation. When you consider using a style or combination of styles, you're considering a number of factors, such as the capability and commitment of the employee, the complexity of the task, the risk involved, other people involved, and resources available, just to name a few. Sort of like how a professional golfer would choose clubs. He would select the right club for the task at hand. For a leader, using the right style or styles is just as critical for getting the desired result."

"I'm a terrible golfer," I said.

"That may be," Ed said, his eyes crinkling. "But we both know that you've got a pretty good understanding of this concept. You wouldn't have gotten as far as you have without it."

"I'm just kidding," I said. "You're right. I get it."

"But maybe you haven't given much thought to the styles at your disposal—the clubs in your golf bag, so to speak. In fact, I'd wager that you settled into one or two styles early in your career, and there you've stayed. And, if that's the case, it's a shame, because they really deserve more thought. Leadership styles have the single most important influence on creating a great working climate for others and for gaining the discretionary effort of others. There's a broad range of how much extra effort somebody can give. It runs the gamut from doing just enough to not get fired, to giving 150 percent a day, every day.

"None of the styles are right or wrong, per se. But the best leaders use the right styles in the right situations to get the right results. And they can use all six of the styles flexibly when needed. What do you think about that, Ben?"

"It makes sense. On paper, anyway. But I'm not sure I buy it as a real-world application. I mean, we all work for CardMedics and the company has its own culture that everyone experiences—both the good and the not so good. So I think leadership styles are maybe a little less important in our company than perhaps in your experience, Ed."

"That is true about the culture—great point. But leadership styles are far more important than you think. Here's why. We agree there is a specific culture at CardMedics that all employees experience. There must be hundreds if not thousands of managers at an outfit that size, right?"

"Yeah, I think we're at just over a thousand."

"Okay, each of those managers creates a working climate their direct reports experience. Furthermore, that working climate drives the discretionary or extra effort that each employee puts forth.

"Wouldn't you say there's an enormous range of effort an employee can devote to the job? For instance, someone who does just enough to barely avoid getting fired, as compared to someone who gives a 150 percent effort."

"Sure. I see it every day at work," I said.

"Now, let's say we both worked at the same company. You work for a great boss. He's competent, capable, and effective, and leads people the right way. He understands and helps you with your problems. Would you say that working for a boss like that would be motivating?"

"Of course," I said, wishing I had the boss he described.

"And let's say I work for a manager who's negative, cynical, punishing, and a blamer. A glass-half-empty kind of guy. Is working for a boss like that motivating?"

"Doubtful."

"And which boss would likely gain the greater discretionary effort from his employees?"

"I think that's obvious: the boss using the positive style," I said.

"Exactly. That's why it's so important for managers to use the right style or combination of styles to get the job done. While we both experience the same company culture, we experience vastly different working climates. And by the way, it doesn't matter if the company is small or large; the leadership styles still have a huge impact on working climate. It's been found that 50 to 70 percent of the working climate experienced can be attributed to the style of the direct manager. Also, the boss sets the example on the preferred leadership styles for the team."

"Okay, I hear what you're saying. The manager makes the difference."

"Right. But there's more. Back to the styles. There are basically six styles. Let me give you the quick overview." He grabbed the napkin and wrote the following:

- Directive—Donald Trump
- Visionary—John F. Kennedy
- Affiliative—Mother Teresa

- Participative—Gene Kranz
- Pacesetting—Bill Gates
- Coaching—Phil Jackson

When he finished, he turned the napkin toward me, put the cap on his pen, and slid it into his pocket. "Let's talk a bit more about each of these." Ed pointed to the first name on the list.

"The directive style requires immediate compliance. Think Donald Trump, his TV show and the "You're Fired!" statements. There is not a lot of dialogue when an order is given. This style is also known as the command and control approach."

"I love that show," I said. "Trump's such a no-nonsense guy. I just sit there watching him work and marvel at the fact that he can get his employees to jump with a single arch of his eyebrow or a quick order or question."

"It is dramatic," Ed replied. "Remember, though, that this style is good in a crisis situation, but the reality is most situations are not crises. Not the best style to use for increasing the motivation of others. This is not a sustainable style. If overused, it will definitely harm working climate."

He pointed to the next name on the napkin. "Okay, let's take a look at the rest. The visionary style focuses on a long-term objective, inviting others to join the leader in the achievement of the long-term goal. Think John F. Kennedy in 1961 when he proclaimed we would have a man on the moon by the end of the decade. Or Martin Luther King's 'I Have a Dream' speech. The visionary style works well in motivating others, particularly when the leader has the credibility to set and achieve the vision. Of any of the styles, this one has the most positive impact on working climate."

I didn't think of myself as much of a visionary, but I could see the benefits of that type of leadership. Kennedy and King inspired millions to make the world a better place. It was hard to argue with the results those two achieved.

"When harmony is required and team morale needs to be raised, the affiliative style is particularly useful. It's a little hard to identify a leader whose dominant style is affiliative, so I'd like you to think of Mother Teresa. She definitely believed people come first. Joe Torre, manager of the New York Yankees, also uses this style heavily. While the affiliative style can raise commitment and discretionary effort, it tends to work best when accompanied with some of the other styles—like the visionary style, for example."

I nodded, letting it sink in.

"When a more democratic, inclusive approach to working with others is needed, think about the participative style. This one is best characterized by Gene Kranz. Remember him?"

"I don't think so," I said. "Should I have?"

"Gene Kranz was the head of Mission Control for the Apollo 13 flight. You were pretty young when the crisis occurred on Apollo 13 in 1970. The service module exploded on board and his team of engineers saved the lives of the three astronauts in the capsule. When astronaut Jim Lovell uttered the now famous line, 'Houston, we've had a problem,' Kranz assembled his team of engineers, scientists, and technicians to develop a solution—when most people were certain the astronauts would never make it back home safely. He declared a famous phrase of his own as he launched the team to fix the problem: 'Failure is not an option.' Over the course of the next few days, his team worked around the clock to jury-rig the craft for the crew's safe return, while the world was tuned in on TV. His team worked together in a participative way to develop a very innovative set of solutions to bring the crew home. Kranz credited this success to what he called the "human factor," a blend of smart minds and hard work. The engineers used their sheer will to find a way to return the

Apollo 13 home safely. Probably the best example of using the participative style you'll find."

"Gene Kranz," I said, nodding my head. "I won't forget his name again."

Ed continued. "Bill Gates is the poster boy for the pacesetting style. This style focuses on accomplishing tasks at a high level of excellence, with the leader setting the pace himself. This style is characterized by turning up the speed, running faster and faster. It requires a high level of motivation and competence to be sustained. While a very useful style in a turnaround situation, if over-relied on and not supported by some of the more positive styles, it will negatively impact climate in the longer term. The style doesn't place a particularly high importance on collaboration; it is characterized by the leader jumping in and taking over situations. That has a tendency to burn people out."

Ed paused, and I could tell he wanted me to give the pacesetting style a little more thought. Was that really what I'd been doing? I admired Bill Gates, sure, but the negative aspects of the style left a bad taste in my mouth.

"When you think of the coaching style of leadership, think Phil Jackson, the head coach of the Los Angeles Lakers. The coach, whether in sports or business, puts his or her focus on the professional development of others first, helping them identify their strengths and weaknesses, learning their aspirations, and providing ongoing support and feedback. When people are open to coaching, this style can have a very positive impact on climate."

Ed pointed to the napkin. "The bottom line on leadership styles is mastering them all and being able to switch styles as conditions require. That creates the best possible working climate that optimizes the performance of your business." He sat back in his chair. "Now there's a mouthful. What do you think, Ben?"

"Fascinating stuff," I said, and I meant it. "I can think of others who use each of these styles, and I can see myself using some of the styles, based on your description."

"What do you think your most used and least used styles are?"

I stared at the napkin for ten seconds or so, and cleared my throat. "The styles I use most often, to be honest, are the pacesetting and directive styles. I do use the participative style from time to time, and probably the visionary style a bit, too. Perhaps not as much as I should. I would say that I don't use the affiliative or coaching styles much at all."

"Based on what you've shared with me the past few days, that doesn't surprise me."

I nodded. "Nope, I don't guess that it would." I took a sip of my soda. "So, when things melted down at your PR firm, what styles did you use most?"

Ed smiled. "I think you can guess. Pacesetting, pacesetting, pacesetting, and directive, directive, directive. I was a bit like a fireman at that time. Two tools. A hose and an ax. Every situation got the hose or the ax, or both. Can you see how this could be a problem?"

"Yeah. I'm starting to." We sat quietly for a couple of minutes, and I stared blankly at the napkin. The ink was beginning to seep into the paper, and I watched as the letters began to muddle together. My work persona was like that, I thought. At first, it seemed crisp and clear, especially to me. But the longer it sat, it all ran together into an indecipherable mess. I thought of my employees, turning to me as they tried to make sense of their jobs, and only seeing confusion and chaos.

Breaking the silence, Ed spoke again. "So you can see how emotional intelligence drives our choice of leadership styles. How leadership style has the biggest impact on working climate. How working climate drives discretionary effort. And do you think, connecting these dots, this chain reaction of emotional intelligence, styles, working climate, and discretionary effort impacts a company's results and financial performance?"

I smiled. "Ed, you're starting to remind me of an attorney. You never ask a question you don't already know the answer to. Yeah, yeah, I'm beginning to see that it has quite an affect on people, climate, and results, and probably on financial performance, too. I'm starting to get it. And I'm starting to see how by using different styles, I might be able to bring these concepts into play with my team."

"Great, Ben. That's excellent." He reached over and patted me on the shoulder. "We can talk more about this if you would like, but I recommend we shift gears and get skiing. What do you say?"

"Sounds perfect," I replied, and breathed deeply. Nobody likes to realize that they're coming up short in an area of their lives they thought they were excelling at, and I felt the weight of the conversation on my shoulders. Releasing the shackles of the heavy discussion and flying down the mountain was exactly what I needed right then, and I couldn't wait to jump into my skis.

"And I've got a surprise. This afternoon, we're going to ski Vail's back bowls. Ever skied in bowls in Minnesota?"

We both laughed at the absurdity of the question. Vail's back bowls were legendary for their huge stretches of soft, dry powder and breathtaking beauty. Most resorts counted themselves lucky to have one bowl; Vail has seven. The anticipation kicked my adrenaline into overdrive.

As we made our way to the ski corral, I prepared for what would no doubt be the most memorable day of skiing of my life. And in the back of my mind, I was beginning to get a sense of how I might do some things differently back at the office.

"Let's do it," I said, and broke into a wide grin.

• • •

Still exhilarated from our afternoon spent maneuvering the dips and peaks of Vail's back bowls, I peeled off my boots and set them on the bench next to me. I leaned back and closed my eyes, reliving the spectacular feeling of freedom that had been unleashed within my body. I felt it tingling from the tips of my fingers to my toes. I was convinced that I could have skied for several hours more. But Ed had another commitment, and I had the conference call with Dan and Jean to make. We decided to meet again in the morning, and went our separate ways.

I walked from the chalet to the shuttle, and the ear-to-ear smile on my wind-blown face must have been shining like a beacon. Families bundled in ski gear–people I'd barely even realized were there–nodded and smiled as I waited in line for the shuttle. A feeling of elation nearly lifted me off the ground.

CHAPTER SIXTEEN

An Out-of-the-Box Idea

After a quick shower and cup of coffee back at the hotel, I dialed into the conference call. Before we started talking, I would have said my day couldn't have gotten any better. After I hung up, I realized I was wrong. I felt goose bumps pop up on my arms, and I paced the hotel room, rehashing the conversation in my mind.

Dan was bold and took charge during the call, a big change from our past two discussions. And the "out of the box" solution he concocted was a unique proposal, to say the least. Worst case, it was a creative idea; a good try. Best case, Dan may have figured out how to save the company from a financial disaster.

But it didn't start out that way. "Okay, here's where we are. Softwrite is going down fast," Dan began, and I felt that familiar sense of dread tug at my feeling of euphoria. He painted a bleak picture. "It's going down even faster than we thought. Right or wrong, the reality is that we've sunk $3.5 million into Softwrite Design Partners. And we all know that if we switch software developers at this stage of the game, we're looking at a six-month delay—or more. If we're forced to delay the product launch, we're not going to make our year, of course, but we're also looking at potential lost revenue of $75 million."

Whatever jubilation I had been experiencing earlier in the day on the mountain was quickly being overcome by the depressing reality of what would lie ahead if we were unable to fix the software problem. It was crystal clear that fixing the bug was pivotal to our new product launch. "I'm with you so far." I sounded like I had swallowed a frog.

Jean spoke up, her voice upbeat. "Okay, Dan. You've let him sweat long enough. Ben, it's not all gloom and doom. Dan may have figured out a way to tackle this problem head on."

"Hey, I'm getting to that," Dan said, and I detected a bit of enthusiasm in his voice. He was obviously excited about what he was going to tell me. "I've been camping out in the Bay Area since Monday. I met with a few potential new software vendors, and had a number of meetings with the Softwrite people. Last night, I took their acting president, Steve Acevedo, out for dinner. During our time together, Steve confided that the firm's cash position is down. *Way* down— under $100 thousand. Due to their over-reliance on a single client that had financial problems of its own, Softwrite was left holding the bag for nearly $4 million of unpaid invoices."

I whistled, knowing full well that a sudden debt of that size had sunk more than a few companies.

"Softwrite's cash burn the past three months has virtually depleted their reserves. Steve has been desperately seeking capital, but he hasn't been able to secure investor commitment. With their unpaid receivables and the loss of their key people, no bank would touch them. I asked for a copy of his business plan, thinking maybe I could try to introduce Steve to some of my own contacts in the financial community."

"Sounds good," I said, and felt the anxious fist unclench from my chest—just a little. "Sounds like you covered all the important topics."

"But wait until you hear where it went from there," Jean said.

"Throughout all our talks, Steve remained confident that if he could just find financiers, he could recover the firm," Dan continued. "But he's worried that he is going to run out of time. If things don't turn positive in the next three or four weeks, Softwrite will be faced with locking the doors for the last time. Steve acknowledged that he felt awful about our problem, and that under normal circumstances, he would have fixed the glitch at no added expense for us. The problem now for Softwrite is financial resources and horsepower. Steve's taken the firm through a series of layoffs as the situation worsened, and the development team at Softwrite is down to just a handful of people."

"He's had to make some tough decisions over the past couple of weeks," I said.

"Yeah. He was clearly disturbed about having to break up his team. He said the group of people that Softwrite had assembled was the best team he'd ever worked with and now, through no fault of theirs, they're gone. If he could secure the financing, he would re-call his laid-off developers. He expressed some bitterness toward his predecessor who had allowed them to get so heavily leveraged with a single client. That guy left the firm and it was up to Steve to sweep up the mess."

"Brutal," I said.

"So that's when I asked him this question: 'If financial resources weren't an issue, how many people would be required to fix our problem and how fast could it be fixed?' Steve thought about it for a while, then estimated six people and, depending on the root causes, probably no more than three or four weeks. The problem was that the majority of the developers on our project were laid off weeks ago. And he was going to need to let two additional developers go this week if he was unable to secure financing. I asked him what he needed to keep the firm afloat. Steve said that $2.5 million would allow them to pay their short-term debts and provide a modest six-month operating expense cushion, while they hunted for new business."

"Sounds about right," I said, breathing deeply and hoping that Dan's idea was as brilliant as Jean made it out to seem.

It was.

"So then it hit me, what if CardMedics loaned Softwrite $2 million? We could work it so it was to be repaid over time—let's say three years. That would allow the firm to bring back their laid-off developers, take care of their other short term payables, and dedicate themselves to fixing our problem. Assuming they're able to resolve the software glitch satisfactorily, and both Steve and I strongly believe Softwrite can, we also have some additional work to throw at Softwrite in the next twelve months." We have two significant products that are nearing end-of-life in the next twenty-four months and, given our need for replacement products which have a significant software requirement, we could consider Softwrite as our preferred vendor if they delivered on *CyberLaser*. Dan and Steve's back-of-the-cocktail-napkin guesstimate showed projects that would cost us about $2.5 to $3 million in software development fees over the next year.

"Interesting," I said, letting it sink in. "A very creative way for our two firms to work together. It'd be a nice carrot for Softwrite. If they can deliver, it would provide them with some reasonable assurance they would have a future revenue stream. And Softwrite's done some great work for us in the past. I don't see any reason why they couldn't continue to work for us again, especially if they're able to deliver on *CyberLaser*." I felt the words tumbling out of my mouth more quickly. "This could be Softwrite's ticket back to solvency and a win-win solution for both companies. Jean, is it doable?"

"Short answer—yes," she said. "While we'll certainly need to negotiate the details of the contract and get it signed, I'm comfortable we can get our short-term problem solved and minimize our longer-term risks. We would provide them a bridge loan of $500 thousand for a month, during which time they would need to fix the software glitch. If they meet that performance stipulation, we'll write them a check for another $1.5 million."

I suddenly found myself standing up next to my bed. The feeling of euphoria that I had experienced on the back bowls was coursing through my body, like helium inflating a balloon. I furiously scribbled numbers on the pad of paper in front of me. "So, for an investment of $2 million, which would be paid back over three years, we could get out of the woods with our *CyberLaser* problem, and potentially avoid a revenue shortfall problem that we forecasted could be upwards of $75 million to our revenue line and almost $35 million to our bottom line for this year?"

This solution seemed to be a no-brainer. After asking a few clarifying questions, I congratulated them both. Assuming Softwrite delivered our solution within four weeks, we would be ready to rock with our launch, with only a minor delay. I authorized Jean to arrange with our CFO, Miguel Hernandez, a transfer of $500 thousand to Softwrite on Friday, provided the lawyers could work out the final terms and details.

"I don't foresee a problem," she said, and I nearly jumped into the air.

"Dan, you knocked this one out of the park," I said. "Way to go."

I could hear the pride in his voice. "Thanks, Ben. That means a lot."

"I'm heading back to Minneapolis on Saturday, and I want you there when I update Mike Cole on the situation on Monday."

"Wow," he said. "That'd be unbelievable."

"You deserve it. Let's talk again tomorrow, but tonight I want both of you to treat your spouses to a celebratory dinner, on me."

We chatted for a few minutes more, and I set the phone down and collapsed onto the bed. As I reflected on what appeared to be a very creative solution to this mess, I couldn't help but see the choices that Ed had enlightened me to at play in the Softwrite matter. Perhaps unbeknownst to Dan, perhaps not, Dan honored the choices perfectly in his interactions with Steve Acevedo.

- Despite my early misguided requests, Dan didn't use fear as a motivation when dealing with the Softwrite president. He was motivated to find a solution, and solutions, I've learned, are rarely discovered until we are out of the "fear" state. Dan was creative in trying to help them solve their problem, so we could get our problem fixed.

- Dan saw the Softwrite president as a person, not a thing or a tool.

- When Dan understood the Softwrite president's predicament, he was supportive of his needs, and receptive, not resistant, to his own sense of what was right. To help us, we needed to help Softwrite. And we could help them at minimal risk or cost to CardMedics. The alternative, tying up Softwrite in the legal system or failing to help them, would have been devastating for both of us.

Bottom line: It sounds like we nailed it. I let out the loudest "Whoop!" I could muster.

CHAPTER SEVENTEEN

Skiing the Gates

I reveled in another beautiful Vail day, with sunny skies and temperatures in the high 30s. As invigorating as the weather was, it was reminding myself of the creative "win-win" solution Dan had come up with that made me feel as though a huge burden was about to be lifted from my shoulders. It wasn't lost on me that the problem was solved with me only peripherally involved and one thousand miles from the office, and it made me consider that the less direct involvement approach may be applicable to other challenges we face at work, too. Maybe less can be more at times, after all.

Ed and I met at our usual spot, at the Lionshead clock tower, and exchanged our morning greetings. I hoped that after a terrific afternoon of skiing through the aspens and pines in ungroomed snow, we would return to the glades in the back bowls to continue our fun. But Ed had a different idea for me for our three-hour ski session.

"Ever skied gates?" Ed asked.

"What do you mean? Like a slalom ski race?"

"Yep, that's what I mean." Ed smiled broadly. He was serious.

"No, I haven't. And to tell you the truth, I've not really had a desire to become the next Bode Miller." The US Ski Team star could hang onto his title, thank you very much.

Ed laughed. "I don't think Bode will be too worried about his position as World Cup champion if you run a few slalom gates. But it could be a lot of fun if we went over to Safari and skied the race course for awhile. The Vail Mountain School ski team isn't on it this morning, so we'll have it to ourselves."

"Boy, I don't know." I visualized myself taking a tumble right out of the gate and slaloming down the hill on my butt.

"It's not too hard; you might be able to do it. It's a different type of skiing to be sure. Think you're up to it, big boy?" he asked in a teasing, cocky sort of way.

Ed was pushing my buttons. He certainly realized I was competitive—how could he not?—and he knew that by throwing down the gauntlet like that, I couldn't help but respond to his challenge. He tossed out the hook and I grabbed the bait. I remembered the rush I'd experienced on the back bowls; maybe the slalom course would deliver that same kind of thrill. "Game on," I finally said, somewhat hesitantly. "Let's get after it."

"That's the spirit, Ben. Variety is the spice of life, you know. Gotta always try new things." He slapped me on the back. "Get ready to get a little snow on your pants."

And so it was to Safari we went, via the Eagle Bahn gondola.

When we disembarked and stepped into our skis, Ed explained some basics and then skied seven or eight slalom gates, flawlessly of course, looking back at me and yelling, "Your turn! Show me what you've got, hot shot!"

I took the first turn pretty easily, getting by the slalom pole with plenty of room to spare. As my speed increased, I struggled with the second turn and got around a bit late. I was totally late completing my third turn, though, and paid the price. It left me in a precarious position with my body facing uphill, causing me to crash into the fourth gate, and knocking me flat on my back. Both my skis popped off.

Ed yelled up the hill. "No worries. It's happened to the best of us!"

"Easy for you to say," I said, spitting snow from my mouth. "You're still standing."

"Got to control your speed. Get yourself up and put back together and come on down here and talk with me."

As I dusted myself off, shook off the spill, and stepped back into my bindings, I decided to ski straight to Ed and forego any additional turns through the slalom gates.

Ed explained the correct slalom technique. "Ben, the key is to let your skis run as freely as possible and use the right degree of edging for your skis to carve–not skid–your turns. You're a bit of a skidder, at times. You'll notice the race course is packed hard, more like your typical Minnesota conditions, than the soft pack and powder we usually find at Vail. So once you get the feel for it, you should do just fine. By the way, you need to keep your eyes focused on not just the next gate, but on the next several gates ahead, otherwise you'll find your butt in the snow. It's kind of like driving in that regard, you know, when you have to watch the action immediately in front of you as well as scan the road for other developments."

I nodded.

"Now, as you approach each gate, angle your body over your edged and weighted outside ski. Your inside shoulder should be brushing the slalom pole aside. Next, as you prepare to turn again, get ready to step onto the diverging uphill ski. Extend up, transfer pressure, then plant your pole and bank into the turn. Then stretch your uphill leg and extend into the turn instead of merely upwards. You transfer pressure to your uphill ski and tilt into its opposite edge in one movement. This is known as 'stepping onto or against the uphill ski.'"

I visualized what he was saying in my mind, concentrating on each step as he described it.

"Finally, steer with carefully controlled outside ski pressure, flex down, and counter-rotate your hips and upper body, your skis around the inside pole. As long as both feet pass through the gate, it doesn't matter if you knock down the pole with your body."

He flashed me an enthusiastic smile. "Now let's try a few more gates. I'll go first to show you the technique and then you copy me, okay?"

Trying to sound convincing, but without much enthusiasm, I mustered a response. "All right."

Again, Ed demonstrated flawlessly.

I skied five or six gates and made it to where Ben was standing. He told me that I was starting to get it, and asked me to ski the remaining dozen gates to the end of the course.

I made it. I completed the course and, believe it or not, had a good time doing it. I felt proud of my accomplishment, and we continued to ski the slalom course for another hour or so, all by ourselves. After a few more runs, Ed pulled up next to me and raised one eyebrow mischievously.

"How about we make it more interesting?" he said, dangling a key between his gloved fingers.

It was the key to the starter's hut at the top of the run. He went inside and turned on the race clock. It was the same type of clock that World Cup racers use, and it would allow us to see the time it took for us to complete the race course. My competitive juices really started flowing, and I got to see my progression over the next hour. Each time I ran the course, I found it easier and easier to link my turns. I wasn't exactly a candidate for the Vail ski team, but I was getting better. My time decreased with each run, too.

I reflected on everything that was going on. I was in the middle of a new skiing experience. I was having a lot of fun, and getting immediate feedback on my performance. It all felt very tangible. This was something I definitely wanted to do again.

At just before noon, Ben said he needed to scoot to another lesson. "Glad you enjoyed skiing the gates," he said. "How about the moguls tomorrow?"

This guy is good, I thought. *He knows how challenging moguls are. He's built my confidence up after the disastrous wipeout, and now tomorrow we ski the moguls.* It was going to be my last day at Vail, and I was as prepared as I'd ever be. What else could I say? "Sure, Ed. I'm putting my safety in your hands. And my family is counting on you, too."

"You'll do fine," he replied. "As long as you keep focusing on those boards of yours."

"I'll be ready," I said. "Hey, one other thing. Since your wife's not getting into Vail until tomorrow night, how about dinner this evening? I'm buying."

"That'd be great," he said.

I was thrilled at the prospect of having two or three hours alone with Ed off the slopes, where we could continue the discussions I had found so enlightening. We agreed to meet at 8:00 p.m. at Chap's Grill and Chophouse, which Ed assured me was the best steak place in Vail.

After Ed's departure, I skied the gates a few more times and decided to practice my slalom turning technique on some of the blue cruising runs. Using the technique Ed shared with me, and turning to make-believe gates, my turns became faster and crisper. I was feeling great!

Thanks for everything, Ed, I thought.

At 2:00 p.m., I decided to take a break for the day. I had some shopping and thinking to do. A lot of questions were racing through my mind that I wanted to bounce off Ed at dinner.

I wound up at the base lodge at Vail Village. From there, I took the short walk to the Golden Bear to pick up a nice gift for Nancy. The Golden Bear is legendary in Vail—a very upscale, elegant women's boutique with its distinctive golden bear jewelry. I bought Nancy a 24-karat golden bear necklace and pendant, a sassy sweater, designer cords, and a rhinestone-studded belt that I knew would look great on her. Stacy, the sales person at the Golden Bear, helped me with the purchases and complimented me for doing well and making someone back home very happy. I was sure she said that to all the husbands who picked up nice things for their wives, but it made me feel good nonetheless.

I smiled in anticipation of Nancy's reaction to the gifts. God, for everything she's done for me, she deserved them. At forty-two, she still has the figure she had in college, and she was going to turn some heads in this new outfit. I thought about taking her downtown to dinner and for some fun at Bellanotte or Zelo when I got home. I was really starting to miss her. Maybe I'd been away from home a little too long.

I finished shopping for Nancy by stopping at Kemosabe, the boot store next to the Golden Bear, and picked up a pair of beige, high-heeled cowgirl boots. *Even though we'll be in Minnesota, she's gonna look like one Vail hottie*, I thought. I stopped at the Christy Sports store and picked up some Vail T-shirts, hats, and fleece pullovers for Jeff and Amber, which I knew they'd love. I missed my kids and wife and was going to be very glad to see everyone on Saturday.

I grabbed the shuttle bus in Vail Village at the covered bridge and headed back to the Marriott for some calls and e-mail before my dinner with Ed. On the ride to the hotel, I began assembling the list of questions that were flittering around in my head.

CHAPTER EIGHTEEN

Dinner with Ed

As I met Ed at the bar of Chap's Grill and Chophouse and we each ordered a drink, I thanked him for agreeing to have dinner with me.

"Ben, are you kidding me?" he said, flashing his trademark grin. "I told you I love hanging out, talking, and having fun with good people. I'm just glad you've enjoyed the skiing and found the other stuff we've talked about useful, too. Your skiing has really taken off this week and it's nice to know you've found some of the ideas we've bounced around to have some value. It's been enjoyable to get you know you."

The hostess showed us to our table. "Ed, it's been better than you know," I said. "First, you're a great guy, a terrific instructor, and an excellent listener. Your instruction—it's surpassed my wildest expectations. But your advice and comments have been what has made it for me. It's great to have another man I can speak with about some of these issues, and you've opened my eyes. I really don't have anyone I can talk with as openly as you and I have talked. I wish CardMedics would hire you to work with our top executives. All of us could sure use the help."

I raised my eyebrows in positive anticipation. "Hope you won't mind if I toss some more questions your way tonight—pick your brain a little?"

"Not at all. We've got as much time as you need. Fire away. But first, could we take a look at the menu? I'm kind of hungry; I've been running gates with you and then was skiing the back bowls with another group this afternoon." He scanned the menu. "I think I could eat that 48-ounce Porterhouse." He winked. "Just kiddin', Ben. Don't want to make you think you'll have to pay for that." We laughed at his joke, but I knew that buying him a hundred Porterhouse steaks wasn't nearly enough to repay him for what he'd given me during the week.

We started with a bottle of the 2000 vintage Sterling Cabernet. Ed ordered the 22-ounce Prime Coute De Beouf, and I decided on the Grilled Colorado Double Lamb Chops. For starters, we both ordered the tomato and onion salads with blue cheese. Their vegetable and side dishes were available a la carte. "I don't think we're finished quite yet," I said, and ordered asparagus hollandaise and garlic mashed potatoes for us to share.

"Let's just agree not to tell our wives—or our cardiologists—about what we're going to eat," he said. But after all, this was a celebration dinner of sorts, celebrating a great week of skiing, a new friendship, and meaningful discussions and reflection at Vail.

Once we placed our orders, I jumped right in. "Ed, I've got a number of questions that are still lingering. I've written them down so I wouldn't forget. I want to get started, because there are quite a few things I'd like to ask you about."

"Shoot," he said, giving me his full attention.

"First, you've told me about losing your job when you headed that PR firm, but you never told me where you worked after that."

"That's because you never asked," Ed replied in a quick-witted, good-natured way.

"Too busy talking about myself and my needs, I guess." We both laughed.

"I'll tell you more about my career, but first let me address something you just mentioned. You said you don't really have anyone you can open up with and discuss what's on your mind. I know that feeling; I was once there myself. And I know from my experience working with the networking group back in Stamford that too many executives–particularly men– don't have someone they can really open up to and discuss what's on their mind in a confidential way. That's an awful thing. Why are we so reluctant to open up and talk with one another about our problems? I guess it's the ego thing."

"It's definitely a challenge."

"If the responsibility of working in a top job isn't enough, it's compounded by not having someone you can bounce ideas off in a safe way that won't come back to bite you. That is very unfortunate. Being the top guy running an enterprise is a tough job. It's lonely. You need someone to talk to. So do me a favor, consider finding a mentor back in Minneapolis, or an executive coach, or another high-ranking executive in a non-competing company—someone you can talk to when you need to, someone who understands the kinds of challenges you're facing and has some experience and perspective. It's not necessary that any of us go it alone. It's actually been shown to be harmful to your health. It adds too much stress and, besides, you make better decisions when you have a partner in collaboration. I know I have. The relationship I built with my mentor David was invaluable. And after he retired from the networking group he founded, I hired an executive coach to keep me on track. It's made all the difference."

"I've got to give this one some thought and find some support in Minneapolis," I said. Ideally, I'd be looking for another Ed, someone who would really listen to me, with plenty of experience helping executives be their best.

Ed took a sip of water. "Okay. That's out of the way. As I told you, it was a long, long road back for me. Took me eighteen months to land another executive position. I had some doubts, to be honest with you, whether I would ever find a job. It was painful. But from pain, if we're willing to open up and reflect on what happened, we can learn from the experience, and from that can come growth. And that was the case for me. Ultimately, I ended up going back into a business development role for a PR firm where a friend of mine had been promoted to president. He and I had worked together about ten years before, and we had several long talks before he offered me the job. Probably to see if I had become as big of a jerk as I'm sure a lot of other people were saying at that time."

Thoughts of my last performance review flickered in my head.

"In any event, I was so grateful to be back working in a role I knew I could be successful in. This time, I took a very different approach to getting integrated in my new job. I really worked on building relationships with the people on my team, with my peers, and with my new boss. I learned that relationships are built on respect, care, and shared experiences. Over time, trust gets developed and increases. In a couple of years, when my friend was promoted to CEO, I was bumped up to president.

"One thing led to another and when my friend retired five years after I started there, I replaced him as CEO. As I mentioned, I retired from that job a few years ago, and started my new career as a ski-bum-slash-instructor in the winter, bicycling tour guide in the summer, professional board sitter, and advice-giver-to-anyone-who-wants-it-and-to-some-who-don't-guy. That's my story."

"Boy," I said. "If I could achieve half of that for myself, I'd be a happy guy."

"It'll come for you, Ben," Ed said. "Oh, one more thing I'm pretty proud of. During the time I was CEO there, we tripled our revenue, almost quadrupled our operating profits, and doubled our number of employees. In spite of the challenging times post-September 11, we didn't lose one person involuntarily. I'm really proud we were able to hang in there, with no layoffs, during that tough period. We started growing again the next year, and I decided it was time to announce my retirement, as it seemed the worst was over. I had groomed my successor and am proud to say the company continues to grow. My successor, Stephanie Collins, is doing a wonderful job. Her team loves her and they are hitting it on all cylinders. It's a better company today than when I left. I had a nice run." Ed smiled and sat back in his chair. "Now, every day is a bunch of nice runs—at least when I'm in Vail."

"Thanks for filling me in on the details," I said. "That's pretty impressive what you were able to do with the firm. And an even more interesting story of your own journey."

"It was more what I didn't do, than what I did. You see, after I hit the wall–which, by the way, happens to most executives at least once in their career–it turned out to be the catalyst I needed to really think through how I'd spend my time, what to get involved in, and what not get involved in. In a nutshell, I learned some valuable lessons on how to add value as a leader."

"Such as?" I asked and pulled my notebook out of my pocket.

"I learned that I needed a new way of *being*, as well as a new way of working. My way of being actually was a choice before behavior. This is where the 'choice' questions I discussed with you a few days ago come into play. A new way of working was what I desperately needed after my leadership meltdown at the PR firm. There are four lessons of a new way of working that, as I look back at my career, are probably worth mentioning. They certainly meant a world of difference for me."

I scribbled furiously. "Tonight I'm the student, so, please, keep talking about the things you think would be useful for me."

"Okay, then. The first lesson learned was that I had to get my own ego under control. When we're motivated by love, our ego is not in control. Something deeper is in control—it's our spirit. Our spirit knows what is right and is not confused by the ego. So, we have to really tune in to hear our spirit, which for many who are always in a hurry, can be quite the challenge. When we are motivated by fear, when we are 'me-focused,' we are motivated by the ego.

"Now, don't get me wrong; as leaders, we do need to have a strong sense of our own capabilities. We have to have an innate confidence in ourselves in order to develop those bold, creative plans for the future and get others to believe in a way that matches our own convictions. What I'm talking about is being driven by ego, being egomaniacal. That had to go. So I identified where my ego had been out of control and I decided to let it go.

"You see, the Old Ed inserted himself into all the important issues at work. I made sure that all the important decisions were made at my desk. I would step on the air hose, slow down the organization, because I had this powerful need to be in control. I knew better than any one else."

"Or so you thought," I said.

"Exactly. I decided to let go of always being seen as in control. I decided to let go of the need to always be right. I let go of the need of always having to win. I let go of being offended by others. I let go of needing to be superior. I decided that I was not my achievements, not my reputation, and not separate from others. I worked hard to let go of these limiting beliefs.

"I learned I had to let go if I really wanted to effectively lead others. I realized we're not disconnected from others—we are all connected. And whatever I could do to strengthen that connection would help me better lead others. I've learned that if you don't strengthen this connection and support other people, your desires will be frustrated. If I connected with others and, together, we sought out possibilities, the sky was the limit.

"Misunderstandings usually result from fear. When people don't understand you, they become fearful. When we put our interests first, we over-focus on self, and ego takes over. This was lesson number one for me: Watch out for signs of ego taking control and squash it, whenever possible."

I kept writing.

"The second lesson I learned was that I would never be smart enough or good enough to go it alone, at least in the leadership roles I envisioned for myself. This meant that I needed to hire the very best people I could find. Once they were on board, I needed to spend a lot of time with them, coaching them, listening to them, working with them, empathizing, and really understanding their needs—then letting go to them, ensuring they had real decision-making authority commensurate with the accountability they had."

"That's a tough one. I've definitely struggled with that," I said.

"Here's the reality. Talented people don't expect their leaders to have all the answers. They don't *want* their leaders to have all the answers, because then it wouldn't be any fun. Business is like a game and solving problems is how you play. It's fun to solve problems—that's what talented people like to do. They will channel vast amounts of energy and effort to do this, if you just get out of their way.

"Now, some managers think you've got to have all the answers and must look perfect at all times. People aren't looking for perfection from their leaders. They're looking for consistency in values, yes, but not perfection. So, it's okay to show you're not perfect, to let your vulnerabilities show through. Coworkers will actually respect and respond to you if you have the courage to show your vulnerabilities. And even if you pretend to have all the answers, they'll see right through you and know you're full of BS anyway. So don't BS them. Your ego says you want to be right, always in control. Resist this temptation. My new way of working necessitated that I encourage my team, coach them, remove obstacles for them, understand what makes them tick, and understand their needs, aspirations, and dreams. Using the right leadership style, at the right time, for the right situations was really important here."

Ed took a sip of wine and rolled it around in his mouth. "Man, that's good. Okay, the third lesson. The leader's job is to get results and to do it with behaviors that sustain the ability to get results for the long term. To get results, I needed to ensure there was absolute clarity about our future and the plans to make the future a reality. Getting the full engagement and support of others requires the leader to be crystal clear about the priorities of the business. It's important to have a robust process where the priorities of the business get established and key people have a voice in them. And to make sure that each player understands how they support the priorities and what is expected of them.

"My experience is that most leaders do a rather poor job of painting a compelling future and ensuring that absolute clarity exists. I worked very hard to make sure everyone was clear about our plans, our standards, their roles, and my expectations. Part of making sure clarity exists is saying no to the fluff stuff that gets in the way of really driving your business. Clarity is key in getting people behind you, getting them really engaged. It's a must for ensuring a winning climate. When everyone is clear, this breeds commitment. Each individual–and the team itself–becomes more capable, and that, in turn, builds greater confidence. And before you know it, you have a virtuous cycle. But it takes a lot of work and the leader's job is never over as far as clarity goes. It's the leader's job to define clarity—it's something only the leader can do."

"This is great stuff," I said, jotting notes as fast as my fingers could move.

"One of the best things a leader can do to create clarity is to have a clear leadership voice," Ed continued. "Think about VOICE as an acronym. It stands for Vision and Values, Optimism, Ideas, Courage, and Educate and Execute."

"Can you go through each of those?" I asked.

"You've got it. Vision. Who wants to follow a leader who doesn't have a clear vision of a better tomorrow? Leaders are people who see a better future, people who are never totally satisfied with today. They've got to make people believe in this vision and they do it through their words, stories, images, and metaphors. If our vision isn't strong, we'll not hold our position when something inevitably comes to shake us. So, 'What's your vision for your business?' is a question that every leader in our organization would hear from me periodically. I expected each to be visionaries in their own right.

"Values. What is it the leader stands for? What is really important? Without strong values, people are moved off course by prevailing winds. What I see a lot of in mediocre managers is not clear values, but situational values—they change with whatever comes up. Clear values give others confidence to act, a roadmap to the clear behaviors the leader and the firm wish to support. While it's important the company has clear values, your people want to know what your own values are, too. Every successful leader I know can rattle off the key values that govern them."

"Makes sense," I said.

"Optimism. The leader must see the glass as more than half full. He's gotta believe the mountain can be climbed, no matter how tough the journey. This optimism is contagious. The leader's optimism or pessimism will spread throughout the company like electricity on wires. Each leader must carefully think about a lot of things: Are you optimistic or pessimistic? Encouraging or discouraging? Are you able to define reality and maintain a sense of optimism so you can view problems as opportunities? Do you let your mood and behaviors affect your work? What percentage of your energy is spent on negative emotions–frustration, anger, resentment, envy–as opposed to the positive emotions that allow you to serve, grow, and create value? How resilient are you? Are you able to overcome setbacks, navigate the daily white water of life, and reach out for possibilities? Beliefs control our behavior. What are your beliefs about work, people, developing others, teamwork, and life? What beliefs are working for you? What are your beliefs costing you? What new beliefs must be developed in order for you to work on purpose?"

Ed paused while I frantically tried to catch up.

"Ideas. Guiding ideas are the central themes we embrace about our business, how our business serves customers and competes, and what must take place for the business to flourish in the future. Defining our leadership VOICE requires precise thinking around our guiding ideas. I asked each of our leaders to carefully think through some key questions for their areas: What must we accomplish? How will we do it? How do we make money? How do we compete? How do we serve others? What challenges is our business facing? Where are we headed? What's our competitive advantage? How will you continue to learn, grow, and perform at your best? How will you assist others to learn, grow, and perform at their best?

"Courage. Having the mental toughness to see reality as it is and demonstrating an ability to critically weigh information, to reason and act decisively. I challenged my direct reports and other leaders to address several issues with their people: How can you use the clarity of your guiding ideas and values to more effectively deal with challenging situations? What have you learned from both your successes and setbacks? I asked them to develop a lifeline, plotting the key events and lessons they experienced during their lives. I asked them: How did these events shape you? What have you learned about yourself? How have these events, learnings, and beliefs given you courage? What are the tough issues you need to confront? What is your greatest business obstacle? What are the difficult discussions you need to have? With yourself, with others? When do you commit to having these discussions?

"Education and execute. Leaders are learners. Leaders educate, instruct, and coach their players, preparing them to execute more effectively. Leaders should be lifelong learners, and use a process of instructing, learning, coaching, and communicating to continue to fine-tune their leadership voice and build clarity. Clarity fosters commitment and commitment drives confidence to act. They need to constantly ask themselves questions. Do those around you understand your vision, values, and point-of-view on leadership? What are the greatest leadership lessons you've learned? What percentage of your time is spent teaching others? On coaching others? What are you doing to keep yourself continually learning, more engaged, and performing at your best? How and what are you learning from others? What is your biggest leadership challenge? What is your greatest business-building opportunity? What are you doing to encourage others to develop their leadership VOICE?

"Defining our purpose and leadership voice takes self-awareness, reflection, time, and energy. The payback for doing this is a congruence and alignment with who you are and what you can be. Each leader is different and I didn't try to use a cookie cutter in developing them. We need to lead, by incorporating some of the lessons and information I've shared with you, in a way that fits us. Defining our individual leadership VOICEs, I've found, helps us do just that. So, if you lead an organization, I believe it's an imperative that you teach others how to discover their own leadership VOICE—but only after you've defined your own."

I looked up after I finished writing, and was surprised to see that our dinner had arrived. Ed was happily munching away on his salad. "We'd better eat before our food gets cold," I said, setting aside my pad and pouring Ed another glass of wine.

After a spectacular meal, Ed continued. "The other big lesson I learned was if I wanted the organization or our people to change, the change had to start with me. I couldn't very well build a case for change and insist on others to change, but not change myself. How hypocritical would that be? But that does happen a lot, I've seen, in business.

"For example, a few years before I retired, our firm was facing numerous challenges—technology, competition, slow-down in economic growth, hardships our customers were experiencing, you name it. These changes required our leadership team to take a much more active leadership role in assisting our younger, less experienced people to get up the learning curve and to personally understand the challenges and pressures they were experiencing. Some of the folks on our leadership team had better coaching skills than others, and we decided that if we were serious about this new direction, we had better get some training on how to effectively coach—and get coaches ourselves. Now, some CEOs might have said, 'This coaching stuff is right for everyone else, but I don't need it.' But I realized that I needed it too and had to be the role model if everyone else was to take this seriously. Whenever change was required, it had to start with me. The reality is that we must continue to learn, develop, and grow at all times in our career. When we stop learning and growing, we've cast our fate."

"Those lessons make a lot of sense," I said. "Who can argue with that? But by delegating as much as you did, didn't you feel out of control? Did your people take advantage of you? Did they let you down?"

"It may sound surprising, but my experience was the more I let go, and the more I let these very capable leaders truly take on the responsibility they were hired for, they exceeded my expectations. Are there problems occasionally and bumps in the road? Of course. But they were relatively few and the headaches they caused were far less painful than the headaches I experienced in my Old Ed state, when I made myself the center of the universe. When I let go, I didn't feel out of control. And by the way, letting others do what they were hired to do doesn't mean you're soft on performance expectations. We set aggressive performance expectations. We challenged ourselves. And since our team knew that I really cared about them and saw them as people, I was able to directly address performance shortfalls on those occasions when someone's performance wasn't where it needed to be."

"How'd you do that?" I asked.

"I met with each of my direct reports individually at least once a month. They ran the meeting, and we discussed the state of their performance in the four work directions they faced: taking care of their customers' needs, taking care of their direct reports' needs, taking care of their peers' needs, and taking care of their manager's needs. In other words— me. These were very, very powerful sessions. They served a wonderful purpose in strengthening our bond, sharing information, and staying aligned. After I instituted these meetings, they proved so successful, we implemented them across the organization. And these were not just 'pat on the back, gee, I'm great' meetings. They needed to spend as much time on what wasn't going so well as they did with the things that were going successfully."

"Talk about improving communication," I said. "Hey, you want to order dessert?"

Ed picked up the dessert menu. "Do you have to ask?"

I went with the chocolate lava cake; Ed had the praline caramel cheesecake with cinnamon bourbon ice cream. We both ordered decaf coffee.

"No need to go overboard," I said. "Might as well order one thing that's not terribly bad for us."

"So where was I?" Ed said. "Oh, yes. Additionally, for each of my seven reports, we had a separate, standing meeting every two weeks, which was their time to meet with me to discuss whatever was on their mind. In reality, these were coaching meetings. I'd ask, 'Joe, what's keeping you up at night?' Or 'Mary, what's the biggest challenge you're wrestling with? How can I better support you?' Again, there was no agenda. It was about whatever they wanted to discuss. Sort of like our meeting, tonight, I guess. If you asked them, those folks would tell you the meetings were incredibly useful to them and ones they looked forward to, I believe."

"This is fantastic stuff," I said. "I can see how incorporating much of what you've said could help me immensely at CardMedics. It helps me see what I've got to do to reposition myself with my leadership team. But I've got a real problem that's facing me when I return to Minnesota. It's a bit uncomfortable to discuss," I said, fidgeting with my fork. "Uh, remember that phone call you overheard on the chair lift Monday? And how I sounded to you? That wasn't exactly out of character for me. In fact, I've gotten some very direct feedback from my team—very recently—that leads me to believe they think I treat them more like things than people."

"Go on, tell me more." Ed's voice took on a softer, more encouraging tone.

"Are you familiar with 360-degree feedback?"

"Absolutely. We instituted a 360-degree leadership assessment process nearly ten years ago at the PR firm. Each leader went through it every other year, and we put our high potentials through the process, too. Receiving the feedback from others–our managers, our peers, our direct reports, customers, and other key people–is critical if we're going to grow, develop, and be our best. It's an excellent process for helping us understand how others see us."

"Yeah, well, I don't know if I'm as excited about the 360-degree process as you are. Here's my problem. CardMedics just completed a pilot program for its senior managers. First time I'd ever been through this kind of process. My feedback was not so great. Very critical. My boss saw the review, too, and he made it clear to me that things must improve from both a behavioral and a results standpoint. He made his point in no uncertain terms: I must significantly change some leadership behaviors or I'm out the door."

Our server returned with our desserts and coffee. Ed's eyes grew wide at the heaping plates of ice cream and cake, and we both dug in.

"And while everything you've shared with me about your crash and career comeback has been extremely useful and interesting," I continued, wiping melted chocolate from my face, "I have a slightly different problem than what you had. Not to say you had an easier time, but it sounds like you got a fresh start with a new firm, a new role, new people—the whole shooting match. That's not my situation. I desperately want to make things work at the company where I am now. But truthfully, I know I'm on thin ice at CardMedics as long as Mike Cole is my boss. I want to make things work, before it's too late. So what would you recommend for my situation?"

Ed pursed his lips. "Well, let me ask a few questions," he said. "What messages did you hear from your feedback?"

"They said I haven't proven that I'm able to effectively bring an executive team together. They called me the Lone Ranger. And they pretty much tore me apart on my leadership approach, saying I treat them as if they're guilty until proven innocent. They commented on what I now know is an overuse of the directive and pacesetting leadership styles. They told me I don't provide any motivation or coaching. Probably most stinging, they said I don't see them as people, but as things or tools to be used."

"Sounds like you need to do some work with your direct reports. Do you think these messages are valid?"

"Yes and no," I said. "I understand that people's perceptions are their reality. And honestly, it hurt to hear that feedback. A couple of things have happened in the last week that are causing me to take this to heart more than I might have otherwise. I'm now thinking I do have a problem with my team. And I think I am a part of the problem. A big part. I'm painfully aware that I have a problem I didn't even know existed. Now, I need solutions.

"There's a little more to it. The day before I was to leave Vail, my number-one supporter and our top performer, a guy I've know and worked with more than ten years, informed me of his plan to resign by mid-year. Craig and I have been in some major battles together, so it came as a total shock. But what was an even bigger shock was the reason he was leaving—me. So that was a shot across the bow, a total wake up call.

"But getting away from the office, the skiing, and our discussions have caused me to do a lot of thinking. Honestly, there have been quite a few times when I have treated others as things or tools. The pressure to perform is really intense at CardMedics, and that's why I push people. Maybe I've justified my treating others this way is because of the pressure. And I now realize, following our discussion, this is a self-rationalization. I also rationalized my actions by telling myself that these are experienced, senior people, and they could take it. Whichever way I slice it, my team has spoken, and they don't see me treating them the way I would want to be treated.

"Interesting, isn't it? I want to be treated a certain way, but then I treat others in a way that is totally opposite. So, now I'm confused. While I recognize I need to develop a different way of being and a different way of leading, Ed, I've got to tell you something: I'm just not sure how to do it."

Our waitress refilled our coffee cups and we both took sips.

"How do I engage my team? If I come back all touchy-feely from my Vail trip, won't this confuse them? Talk about lack of clarity. And won't they see me as a phony? Won't they be skeptical about whether I can make positive change? And that assumes that I can even *make* positive change, which I'm not so sure I can." I set down my fork and took a breath. "Ed, help! Where should I start? What would you do?"

"What do you feel is the right thing to do?"

"That's the question I'm wrestling with. I feel like I need to talk with my team, probably as a group and probably also as individuals. God, this whole situation is making me feel awful just thinking about it. I know I haven't treated them like I'd want to be treated. I'm feeling guilty and a little ashamed for being such an idiot. In a way, I wish I could start over."

Ed jumped in. "That's understandable. And, by the way, good work about being so open about your challenge. Being able to articulate the problem gets you half way toward fixing the problem. That's really a healthy first step.

"I have a few ideas for you. But I want to address these guilt and shame feelings head on. It's been my experience that very, very few leaders are motivated to be deliberately cruel to people and treat them as things. Yeah, there are some jerks out there who just don't care. But they are a small minority and that certainly doesn't describe you. The very fact that we're having this discussion shows you care. And as I've gotten to know you this week, I'm convinced you're a good person who wants to do the right thing."

"Thanks for that. So, what should I do?"

"First, I'd suggest you give yourself a break. Guilt and shame are such powerful and negative emotions. Be easier on yourself. You didn't start out wanting to be rough on people, I'm going to guess. But while we're busy and stretched, things happen; we become emotionally numb if we're not careful. We can get caught up in it." He smiled broadly and gestured to the twinkling lights of Vail outside the restaurant windows. "Today's a new day; every day offers the opportunity for a recovery. So why don't you try to fix things with your existing team? I think you've been a lot like a boiling frog—know that story?"

"I don't think so," I said. "But it sounds intriguing. Let's hear it."

"A scientist somewhere, the story goes, said that if you place a frog in a pot of boiling water, it will hop out to save itself. But if you put the frog in a pot of water that's at room temperature, and gradually turn up the temperature of the burner, the frog will be oblivious to the incremental increase in heat, stay in the pot, and ultimately perish."

Ed sipped at his coffee.

"So, maybe the 'pot' you've been in has gotten progressively warmer. And now it sounds like you've realized it, and decided it's time to hop out. It's your choice. You can change if you want. And if you decide to make a change, you have to do it without hanging onto guilt about the past. You were doing as well as you could. What's important is that it sounds like you now are at a place where you need to make a change. Is that right?"

"Yeah. I'm committed to making some changes. It's just how I do it that is still a question. Thanks for the comments—they do make me feel better. But I'm still wondering what I should do with my team."

"Ben, you're awfully impatient," Ed said, smiling and scraping the last bit of cheesecake from his plate. "I told you I had a few ideas for you. Let me give you a thought that may help you specifically solve your conundrum. Based on all of your reflection and learnings this week, if you could focus on two specific things that would help you be the best leader possible, what would they be?"

"Only two? I have about ten things I should focus on," I said.

"Let's limit it to just a few. You are much too busy to focus on ten areas for development. Besides, if you do a good job of picking just a couple, those two new behaviors or styles will spill over and help you improve in some areas that are of lesser importance. Think about two. Think about the eighty-twenty rule. What's the twenty that gets you the eighty?" Ed asked.

"Okay, that's workable." I rolled through the options in my mind. "Let's see. I think they would be: one, develop stronger relationships with those I depend on at work; and two, use the right leadership styles to create clarity, a healthier working climate, and get better results."

"Great! Based on what you've described for me, those would be two big wins. And they both are very doable. So here's my idea. Why not get your leadership team together and tell them you received your 360-degree feedback report just before you left on your trip. You've used the week for reflection and have decided you need to make some changes in how you lead. By the way, you also thank them for responding to your 360 and for their honest feedback. You can tell them as you thought about where you should put some development focus, you settled on two areas. And then tell them about the things you just mentioned: Developing stronger relationships with people and using the right leadership styles to create greater clarity, a healthier climate, and better results."

I nodded. It all made sense.

"Now here's a different twist. You've already gotten the feedback that these are areas that need focus. So for now, you may want to consider a request for clarification from the team and each individual. But instead of asking for more feedback and examples of where you could have done a better job on these two areas for development, why not ask for feedforward?"

"Obviously I'm familiar with feedback. And right now, not a big fan of any more of that. What do you mean by feed-forward?"

"Feedforward is advice that focuses on the possibility of the future, not on the mistakes and screw ups of the past," he said.

"That sounds a whole lot better than feedback," I said.

"Feedforward is based on the reality that we can't change the past, just the future. Anyone who knows something about the task can give you feedforward, whereas people have to know you to give you feedback. Feedforward, from my experience, is not taken as personally as feedback. And best of all, it can cover almost all of the same material as feedback."

"This is definitely sounding better. So how would feedforward look for me?"

"You would say something like this: 'I've gotten a lot of feedback on areas where I might improve. Two areas that would seem to have a big impact if I improved my performance are developing stronger relationships with those I depend on at work and using the right leadership styles to create clarity, develop a healthier working climate, and get better results. So where I need your help is by giving examples of what it would look like if I did an excellent job of seeing each of you as people at all times. What would a stronger relationship look like? Similarly, what kind of leadership styles or behaviors would you experience from me, going forward, that would lead to a healthier working climate? Describe for me what that would look like.'

"From my experience, they'll tell you what they are looking for. You can have this discussion with your full team when you are all together, you can do it individually, or you can do it both ways."

"Nice," I said, taking a final swig of coffee.

"Now here's the kicker. To help make the change stick for you, to keep you honest on your change plan, and to help change their perceptions of your behavior as you are getting better, you let them know that you will be following up with them every four or six weeks for the next six months to ask how you're doing and to seek additional feedforward. We had excellent experience using feedforward at the PR firm following up the 360-degree feedback. In fact, when we used follow-up surveys to see if our managers were really following up with their development advisors to seek feedforward, the results showed the managers who made the greatest improvement were those who frequently followed up. Those who were seen as improving less didn't follow up as frequently."

"So, you're saying I need to ask my direct reports to keep an eye on how I'm doing?"

"Precisely," Ed said. "And let me tell you why. It's human nature to be skeptical of others' claims to change. By following up with others regularly on your progress, you'll do a couple of things. First, you'll show them you are really committed to changing behaviors. It's not a flash-in-the-pan, one-time event. Second, if you've been following up regularly and slip along the way, people will be much more likely to give you the benefit of the doubt, versus thinking something like, 'There goes Ben, back to his old tricks. He was never really committed to change, anyway.' They will be far more likely to think, 'Ben has asked us for suggestions and has made progress on his personal development. It looks like he's having a tough time. I wonder if something is up. What can we do to help him?'"

Ed finished his own coffee. "So, what we've learned is that in parallel with changing certain key behaviors, we also work to change the perceptions of others. These two go hand-in-hand."

"Ed, thanks," I said. I sat back heavily in my chair. I was stuffed, both with amazing food and even more amazing knowledge. "These are excellent ideas for me to get reconnected with the team. I need to think more about it, but I'm beginning to see how I could put these techniques in place as soon as I get back to Minneapolis. Thanks a ton."

I looked at my watch. "Man, it's 10:30 already. Where did the night go? I know I need to let you go soon. But I've got one last question to ask. You seem like a very together, happy guy. What's your secret?"

"Ben, I feel like I'm the luckiest guy in the world. I wouldn't trade places with anyone. I do have a few things I've learned about this, too. But I've got to ask a favor. I'm supposed to ski bumps with you tomorrow morning, starting at 9:00 a.m., and I'm beat. Could we pick this up tomorrow during our time together?"

"Absolutely. I'm excited to get together tomorrow to learn from the master—both to learn to better ski the bumps and maybe how to navigate the other bumps in life, too."

"It's a deal. See you at 9:00 a.m. Thanks again for dinner. It was really great. Remember, we're going to meet at Vail Village to get closer to the best mogul runs."

And with that, Ed said farewell for the night. I paid the bill and walked back to the hotel under a clear sky with a million stars overhead.

CHAPTER NINETEEN

Practicing Mindfulness

When I arrived at Vail Village, Ed was already there. "I'm still stuffed from last night," he said, patting his stomach. "Thanks for a great dinner. How are you doing today?"

"Getting better and better," I said. Vail Village was alive with activity, and the sun made the snow along the streets glimmer like diamonds. "That was a terrific evening. Thanks again for sharing all that with me last night. You've given me a lot to think about."

"I'm glad you're getting something from our time."

"That's an understatement, Ed."

He smiled. "So here we are, the last day of skiing. Let's talk about our game plan for today." He clapped his hands together. "Okay, here's what we want to do. Let's walk over to Riva Bahn lift with our stuff. We'll then take the Northwoods chair lift and ski Prima, Pronto, and Log Chute."

I definitely recognized the names of those runs. Vail's mogul skiers measure their prowess by how many "PPLs"– Prima, Pronto, and Log Chute runs–they've done in a day. I was excited to ski with the "big boys," but there was something I wanted to do before we got started.

"Ready to run the bumps?" Ed asked. "Become a true Vail bump skier for one day?"

"Just about," I replied. "But I've been thinking since last night, and I'd really like your thoughts on a couple of matters.

Okay if we grab a cup of coffee and talk for a bit first? You know, continue our discussion from last night? I'm ready to ski whenever we're finished."

"No problem, Ben, this is your time. Whatever works best for you. I don't have my next lesson until 1:00 p.m., so we've got the time. Let's grab a cup and we can jump in."

We headed to the Starbucks kiosk and loaded up with our usual. We found a couple of chairs and table in the back where we had some privacy, and settled in.

"So, I need to do some fence mending with my direct reports," I said, blowing on my coffee. "I acknowledge the need to do this, more with some than others, but I need to speak with everyone on the team, for certain."

"Good first step," Ed said.

"In particular, there are two people with whom I'm going to need to get a few things straight. I admit I haven't always been the enlightened leader with them, but they've screwed up, too, and we've got to have a talk and reach a common understanding before we can move forward."

"Sounds like you've got a good handle on what you've got to do," Ed said.

I nodded. "But I'm not sure how to do it. I acknowledge that I've been particularly hard on both of these guys. One of them is my direct report you overheard me speak to on Monday—Dan. Now don't get me wrong, these guys have messed up on occasion, too. So while I'm willing to take your advice from last night and engage both of them with the ways I'm trying to change and become a better leader, I need to get on the same page with them. Sort of a clearing of the air. I know there are things I need to do better, but there are some things they need to improve on, too. So, any suggestions on how I go about communicating that to them?"

"I hear you, Ben. It's rarely a one-way street when people have issues professionally, and if everyone is going to be their best, it's important that both you and your players take a long, hard, objective view of yourselves, the status of your relationship, and how the future might look differently. So it sounds to me like you need a new working agreement with a few of your guys."

"That's it, exactly."

"Well there's a way the two of you can create a new future together." He took a sip of his coffee. "Think about the relationship as a conversation. It needs to take place in the context of a shared, two-way discussion. A real dialogue, not a monologue. When you think about it, our relationships are really about conversations. Are our relationships working for us, or are they breaking down? The answer to this typically depends on the quality of our conversations. We need to speak and listen to others with our full attention, as though every conversation is the most important one we've ever had."

I nodded. Ed obviously knew what he was talking about here. Each time we got together, I marveled at how he made me feel as if we were the only two people in the room.

"I'll give you a few ideas for a conversation that's designed to build a bridge to a better future. A new kind of dialogue designed for improving your relationships."

"That's just what I'm looking for," I said.

"Okay, rebuilding a relationship can be done, assuming you both are willing. The place to start, of course, is by seeing Dan as a person. Using some specific questions will get you on your way. Let's start with how you see and behave toward Dan. I've got a series of questions you can first reflect on yourself, and then ask Dan. Let's do a little real-time role playing. I'll ask you a question and then you respond. Ready to go?"

"Fire away."

"What's your view of the ideal working relationship with Dan?" Ed asked.

I thought about it. "Well, Dan must be more accountable for his actions. He needs to be more action-oriented. He needs to think and act more strategically. He must take ownership and look for ways to improve without being pushed by me. And he needs to collaborate more effectively, especially with our marketing team and me."

"Fine," Ed said. "So what are the one or two most pressing issues in your working relationship that must be addressed with Dan right now?"

"Probably the accountability-ownership and collaboration aspects. If he stepped up in these areas, I'd be very happy and he'd be a more valuable leader," I said.

"Excellent, Ben. You're getting it. Now, as you've worked with Dan in the past, have you demonstrated any unproductive behaviors in your relationship with him?"

I reflected on that one for awhile. "Yes, without question. I've been overly critical of him. I haven't made the effort I could have to connect with him. Also, I probably haven't coached or really supported him. Honestly, I wrote him off early."

"A thoughtful, honest admission," Ed said. "Good for you. Can you commit to some new behaviors going forward in your relationship with Dan?"

"I can commit to getting to know him better. I can try harder to understand the world from his perspective, be less judgmental and blaming. I think I can do this by spending more time with him and using the coaching and participative styles of leadership we discussed a few days ago."

"Okay, sounds like a great plan. We both know, however, that relationships are characterized by peaks and valleys. So I always say, expect the unexpected. You and Dan may very well have setbacks. Probably will. When you and Dan have a difference of understanding in the future, how would you suggest this be addressed?"

"We should speak about it immediately. No waiting around if there is something we've got to talk about."

"Good, Ben. Now what else is needed to ensure the success of your relationship with Dan? What should you and Dan do to ensure that change sticks?"

"Be open to discuss any issue privately in a real-time way. I'd be interested to hear what Dan answers this question. I also think we need to discuss how we're doing on a regular basis, probably every sixty days or so. A reality check of sorts. What's going well and not so well?"

"Sounds like you're in a good spot to fix your relationship with Dan. Do you see how if Dan also discussed his views to these questions with you, this could be a powerful way to gain another chance at making it work a whole lot better?

"Yeah, I can see how this could help," I said. "I do indeed."

"But in order for this to work, both parties have to be willing to bury their hatchets. The discussion needs to be held in a supportive way where you both are active and equal partners. Sometimes that's tough to achieve when you're working with a direct report. But that's your challenge, Ben, to make sure Dan, or whoever else you're having the discussion with, feels that you are genuine in your support of them. That you're seeing them as a person, not a thing. It takes more than words. It takes actions, too. It's up to you."

"This is good." I pulled a note pad from my pocket. "Can you go over those questions one more time?"

"Yep, here we go." And he listed them. "One: What's your view of the ideal working relationship with this person? Two: What are the one or two most pressing issues in your working relationship that must be addressed with this person today?

Three: Have you demonstrated any unproductive behaviors in your relationship with this person? If so, what needs to be done? Four: What new behaviors are you committed to going forward in your relationship with this person? Five: When you and this person have a difference of understanding in the future, how would you suggest this be addressed?"

"Excellent," I said, jotting down the last of the questions onto the pad. "That will really help me. Now let's shift gears. I've been amazed at your attitude from the second we met, and I've been meaning to ask you about this for a while. You're human and there must be days when you don't feel at the top of your game. How do you stay so upbeat? You seem very happy. What's your secret? You have such great perspective on life. Are there times when you aren't so optimistic? When things aren't going so well?"

Ed laughed. "Sure. I experience challenges like everyone else. But the short answer is happiness is a choice we each make. So, I choose to be happy. Daily. I'll even let go of being right at times, in order to be happy. It's much more fulfilling to be happy than be right, I've found. But there's more to it than just deciding to be happy, as important as that decision is. Getting to know myself has been key. Getting my mind, body, and heart in sync has been really important. It's not the easiest thing in the world to do, but it's certainly worth it."

"I've come this far," I said. "A little extra work doesn't scare me."

He gave me a quick wink. "No, I don't suppose it does. What you've got to remember is that everybody has problems. Everybody suffers loss and sometimes has emotions and thoughts that aren't altogether positive."

"Even you."

"Yep, even me. We haven't talked about this, but I lost my daughter Kathleen to breast cancer six years ago."

I set down my coffee cup. "Ed, I'm so sorry."

"Thanks. It was a tough time for Sally and me. No question. And I miss Kathleen every damn day. But even with all that, bad days–the days when I wallow in the past or worry about the future–they're more the exception than the rule."

"So how is that the case? How in the world can you be sitting here, smiling, after everything you've been through? Your daughter's illness, getting fired from the PR agency? How have you been able to not only survive, but actually thrive?"

"Well, it's a number of things. Certainly a lot of what we've already discussed has played a big role, particularly when I was working full-time and leading people. But the real difference that keeps me centered, I believe, is what my wife calls 'Ed's daily routine.' It's something I've done now for over ten years, and I do it just for me. I do it every day and it keeps me in sync. I couldn't imagine a day now that I didn't do my routine."

"Exercise?" I asked.

"I do incorporate daily exercise into my routine, yes. If my body's healthy, I find my mind is a little clearer. But it's so much more than that."

"I'm in the market for a new routine," I said. "I'm in a place now where I want to make some real strides as a person and as a leader. I'm motivated and don't want to lose this motivation. I'm a little nervous, too. I'm thinking maybe I won't be able to make some changes or they won't be sufficient or as quick as they need to be. So any pearls of wisdom would be appreciated. Can you let me in on your routine?"

"I can, but we'll need more coffee; this might take a while." I grabbed our cups and refilled them at the coffee bar.

"Thanks," Ed said, wrapping his hands around the cup and breathing in the steam. "Ben, there are many paths to getting to know ourselves better, for building our self-awareness. And, to tell you the truth, I can't give you the key to helping *you* become more self-aware, because you have those keys within you. But I'll tell you about my routine. I've really only shared it with a few people. No guarantees that it will work for you. Or that you are ready for it. But if you really want to hear it, I'll take some time to explain what I do."

"Please, go on."

"Okay, I think a challenge for most everyone, me included, is slowing down so we can be in the present. We have a tendency to plan and look ahead to the future. We also have a tendency, at least many of us do, to spend a lot of time on analyzing the past and re-hashing the events of yesterday. Wouldn't you agree?"

"Sure," I said. "Most of the thoughts that fly through my head are about ways I'd have done something differently, or worrying about what's to come."

"Right. You've heard the saying, 'The past is history, and tomorrow is a mystery?' So that leaves the only time we have as the present. While we need to look at the past and learn from it so we can do things differently now, we have to avoid being overly fixated on what's past. And we certainly want a bright future and need to put in the plans to make that happen, but we need to be reminded that the only time we really have is now." He tapped his finger on the table to drive home the point. "Right now. Today. But focusing on the future can be like a narcotic. We plan and plan and plan and realize we're not living today. How do we make now–this moment, the present–the best it can be? That's the challenge, and it's an ongoing one for most of us. We are habitual creatures and tend to work against being aware in the moment.

"So that's where my daily routine comes into play. It helps me a great deal with being more aware of the present moment. It has also helped me see the interconnectedness of things, of being able to see issues in a deeper way, more than just cause-

and-effect. This routine I use, I know, has helped me develop a greater understanding of myself and others. It's allowed me to move away from day-to-day struggles and grasp the potential of possibilities. It is the best way to build self-awareness that I know. Anyone can do it if they're willing to be disciplined. But you've got to be ready for it."

"Okay, enough with the build up," I pleaded. "I'm getting really curious. Spill it!"

Ben raised an eyebrow and leaned forward. "What if I told you it was not something so much you do, but about something you *are*?"

"You are losing me, Ben. This is sounding squishy."

"What if I told you the core of my daily routine is over 2,500 years old? What would you think, then?"

"I think I'd be relieved to hear that it's not Pilates, spin cycling, or some other New Age exercise or diet plan. And if it's so good and so old, how come I don't already know about it?"

"Before I share it with you, I need you to agree to one thing. I'm going to ask you not to prejudge my routine until you give it a try. Are you okay with that?"

"Deal. Like I said, I'm ready for some big changes in my life. Let's hear it."

"Okay, here goes. The core of what I do is practice mindfulness." He smiled contentedly, as if he had just revealed the secret of the universe, right there in Starbucks. "Ever heard of it?"

I paused, and the blank look on my face must have told Ed that I had no idea what he was talking about. "What in the world is mindfulness?" I finally said. "Is this like some Eastern mystic cult thing? Is this like meditation, chanting, or what? Will I have to ride a llama in Tibet or something?"

Ed gave a belly laugh. "Ben, let me assure you that what I do is far from a cult-like ritual. It's practiced by people all over the world, people from all the major religions, people from all walks of life. Yes, mindfulness does incorporate meditation, but it's more than meditation. Meditation is just a tool that we can use to become more mindful." He looked at me and smiled. "So are you ready to hear more?"

"Frankly, this doesn't sound like something I would do." I sipped at my coffee. "But, I'm intrigued. You seem to be pretty impressed with what it's done for you. And it's obvious you've got some secret the rest of us have no idea about. How does it work?"

"The first step is my sense of being. We're called human beings for a reason. But with the pressures we face–in working, raising families, attending to our 'doings'–it's easy for us to forget we are human beings and not 'human doings.' The source of our thoughts is our being-ness. So every day, at least once a day and ideally twice, I get myself quiet and centered. It's been said that we have sixty thousand thoughts a day that run through our mind. By getting ourselves centered and our minds quieted, perhaps we can find some quiet space between our thoughts. I make a conscious effort to get away from doing for awhile, when I meditate."

I pictured Ed wearing a bright red tunic, sitting on a mountainside, chanting and playing little cymbals with his fingers. *Meditation?* I thought. *Is he kidding?* I could feel my brow scrunching up into an expression of skepticism.

"Mindfulness is about centering ourselves in the present moment," he said. "We do this by sitting down, taking a deep breath, and focusing on our breath. This is breathing meditation. It's about waking up and living harmoniously with our internal and external worlds. Mindfulness helps us be in touch. It helps us control our ego. It requires effort and some discipline because our neural circuitry is predisposed to living life on the fly, on autopilot if you will, and following the comfortable habits we've practiced for so long."

Ed inhaled deeply and slowly, then exhaled. "So, when we meditate, we focus on our breath. We inhale and breathe in the present moment. We exhale and let go of the past. During our exhale, we literally let go of the person we once were. While we may not see it immediately, to be totally in the present, which is what mindful meditation absolutely requires, means we relinquish the past and the future."

I watched his face as he closed his eyes and breathed in and out. I fidgeted and looked around to see if anyone was staring at us. Ed seemed unconcerned.

"Mindfulness is a pathway to our internal wisdom. Meditation is the exercise that helps us be more mindful. It really is the pathway to personal and spiritual growth. This inherent wisdom we possess can only be reached through meditation." He opened his eyes. "Yet there's a paradox here. When we meditate, our objective is not to improve ourselves, but to recognize where we are in the present moment. I like to think of it as a way of being versus something we do. Meditation is the pathway to self-awareness, the way to ensure we grow as people."

"Okay, when you paint it like that, it does sound a little less granola-crunching. It sounds like it's had quite an impact on your life. So how do I do it? What's the trick?" I asked.

"There's no trick at all. It's simple to do, but not easy. Simple, because it's as basic as breathing. But it's not easy, because our ego doesn't want us to gain insights by tapping into our inner wisdom. Your ego will invent a thousand reasons why you shouldn't meditate, why it won't work for you, why it's not a tool for a busy executive to use. And so on and so on. So to see if it can benefit you, you need to give it some time and try your best to be non-judgmental about the practice of meditation or the results you immediately receive.

Trust me, if you meditate daily for thirty days or more, I think you'll see how it can benefit you."

"So, what—do I get down on the floor every morning and sit with my legs crossed?"

"There are all sorts of ways to build your self awareness. Some people draw a long bath and light a few candles. Some people go on long walks with their dog. I've found that it's most helpful for me to get out of the office setting and meditate, so that's why I do it in the morning before I leave the house. It's tough to meditate in your office when your assistant could come bursting through the door at any second with an urgent message."

"How about me? What would you recommend for me?"

"Let's go over the basics, and then, once you give the no-frills version a try, you can adapt the technique to the best way that fits you and the way you live."

"Sounds good," I said.

"We start by sitting in a chair with a straight back. We don't want to set rigidly, but in a way that we're sitting in dignity. A way of sitting that is comfortable to us, without our body being in conflict. We then bring attention to our breath. Our breath is our reference point. You notice the flow of your breath as it comes and goes through your nostrils. Don't worry about controlling your breath, just notice it. When we meditate, we don't want to fight with ourselves, so it's okay to move if we don't feel comfortable. Now each time you breathe in or out, note 'in' or 'out' to yourself. Like a soft, soothing voice. Watch your tension disappear. Deep breathing and tension are incompatible. You with me so far?"

I nodded. "I'd be afraid I wouldn't get into it. I'd just spend the time worrying about the meeting I've got tomorrow or the argument I had with my wife the week before."

"That's natural," Ed said. "Let sounds and thoughts pass. Don't try to fight them. You can notice them coming in like waves on the ocean. The wave comes in and goes out. When your mind wanders, and it certainly will, label your thoughts quietly to yourself as 'thinking.' Your thoughts will go in and out like waves. Thoughts will enter your mind; it's natural. The thoughts may get stronger or weaker, but they will fade away. Try your best not to judge your thoughts. Just acknowledge them.

"Return to your breath and focus on the rhythm of your breath. The coolness, tingling, vibration, and expansion of your chest that breathing causes. Sense it carefully. Focusing on our breath allows us to connect our mind, heart, and body to the present, helping us get in sync. Each time you are distracted by a sound or a thought, bring your focus back to your breath."

I let the soothing rhythm of Ed's words wash over me and could actually feel myself beginning to relax, just by listening to him speak.

"When we sit still and focus on our breathing, our mind, heart, and body begin to open," he continued. "We get in touch with aspects of ourselves we've perhaps not been aware of when not in meditation. This opening can't be forced. Give it time. Whenever you feel ready to stop, open your eyes and carry mindfulness with you." He exhaled slowly. "Ready to give it at try?"

"Here?"

"Yep, here."

Self consciously, I did a quick scan of the area near our table. Everyone seemed to be engrossed in their own conversations. I hesitated, then nodded. "As long as you're sure we're not sitting in a 'no transcendental meditation' section."

"Wait until you try it, smart guy. Let's just shut our eyes and focus on our breathing for a little while. Try to forget about time."

I sat straight in my chair, closed my eyes, and began to breathe. After what seemed like just a few minutes, I opened my eyes to see Ed smiling at me. Something had happened while I meditated, but I wasn't sure what it was. I felt a sense of relaxed calmness. Tranquil and peaceful. It was as if I'd just awoken from an especially revitalizing catnap.

"How long was I meditating?" I asked.

"Almost ten minutes."

"Whoa."

Ed smiled and said, "Once you become accustomed to meditating, you'll feel so good about this discipline that you won't want to miss it. So keep it going for thirty days, twenty minutes or so at a time, and just see what happens. Try starting your day with meditation, when your mind is most open, and see the shift for yourself."

"I'll give it a try. I know I gave you a hard time about it, but I've got to admit I like this feeling. I feel—I don't know—refreshed."

"Excellent," Ed said. "Three other aspects complete my routine. Let me give you a quick rundown, and then let's hit the mountain. First, each morning, before I begin my meditation, I think about and appreciate the things that are most important to me—my family, my friends, my relationship with my wife, my health, my life, the ability to do what I love to do. Starting the morning in an appreciative mindset helps me get ready for the day.

"Part of my appreciation is to also focus on my purpose, and that is and has been for quite some time to enrich the lives of other people by being a contribution to them. I actually meditate on how I can be more of a contribution to others.

Whether it's back in Connecticut with my grandkids, guiding bike trips or ski instructing, talking with an old friend, or meeting a new one, I look for small ways that I can be a contribution to that person."

"I'll say you do," I said, sipping the last of my coffee. "If you have half the impact on other people as you did on me this week, you certainly are being a contribution to others. It's really been unbelievable."

"Thanks, Ben. You're kind to say that. I find being appreciative for what I have, reminding myself what I intend to do with my life, and practicing mindfulness meditation daily have worked for me. They're tactics that help me to stay in the present and live a more fulfilling life. They quiet my ego, help me focus on what is important, and allow me to keep things simple. Thanks for letting me share this with you."

"Ed, you're the one who should be getting the thanks. It's really been amazing."

We stood up and collected our coffee cups. "Well, you came here to ski," Ed said. "It's your last day in Vail. Let's go hit the moguls."

"Just try and stop me," I said, and we headed toward the mountain.

CHAPTER TWENTY

The Moguls

Friday was yet another day that completely exceeded my expectations. Once again, Ed delivered with expert advice on trying some new things with my team and by sharing his daily routine of practicing mindfulness with me. He even got me to try meditating—in a Starbucks, no less.

The mogul skiing was much more enjoyable than I had anticipated. Ed gave me the basics on skiing the bumps: hitting the top of the mogul, rotating my skis at the moment of minimum friction, transferring weight to my outside ski, and steering down into the hollow area between the bumps. Do it again, and again, and again.

He taught me the essence of mogul skiing is to make the terrain work for you, not against you, a feat easier said than done when you're looking down at a field of moguls, some of which were large enough to hide an SUV. He spoke of the need to choose a line through the moguls and follow it, similar to charting a direction in business that you think will lead to the best result and sticking with it. Interesting parallel!

We wrapped up the lesson, and I was both exhilarated and exhausted from another fabulous day of skiing. But the strongest thing I felt was a pang of sadness. I needed to say goodbye to Ed.

I knew I couldn't possibly thank him for everything he'd done for me. If his intention was to make a contribution to the lives of others, well, he certainly did so in a big way with me. This guy was too good to be true. I wondered how many others were lucky enough to have had a similar experience with him.

"Ed," I said, extending my hand. "I've been going over everything we did, everything we talked about this week, and I'm just so grateful."

He shook my hand enthusiastically. "You've really come a long way with your skiing. It truly has been a pleasure getting to know you, Ben."

"I'm pleased with the progress I made on the slopes, sure. But it's everything else that I'm still reeling over. You helped me change my life this week, Ed. That's not something I take lightly. Just know that I'll appreciate what you've done for me for the rest of my life." We talked about getting our families together in Vail soon, and Ed wished me a safe trip home.

"So, one last question before I leave," I said. "You think I'll be able to put all this stuff we talked about to work? Do you think I'll be able to make it happen?"

"I don't think you will," he said, his eyes twinkling. "I *know* you will."

We hugged, and went our separate ways.

I continued to ski for a few hours, and was thrilled to discover that my newfound skills didn't follow Ed off the mountain. His instruction had stuck with me. Even without him by my side, I was succeeding. By the time the lifts closed just after 3:00 p.m., I was completely worn out.

Back in my room, I desperately wanted to take a nap, but decided this would be a good time to give the meditation technique Ed shared with me another try instead. He said that he found a good meditation can take the place of several hours of sleep. *Let's put it to the test*, I thought.

Concentrating on my breath, I marked the inhales with "in" and exhales with "out." Doing it brought me quickly to a more relaxed state. When thoughts came into my mind, I labeled them "thinking" and then went back to focusing on my breath. I found the meditation quite enjoyable. When it felt as though I had enough meditation, I opened my eyes and was pleasantly surprised that I had been meditating for twenty-eight minutes. Given the way my mind usually wanders, it was more than a little surprising I was able to stay with it for so long. I felt a sense of warmth and calmness that left me refreshed and stress-free. Much more refreshed and clear-headed than if I had taken a nap. If I had any hesitation about meditation, I was now sold. This was a routine I needed to incorporate going forward.

I decided to spend my last evening in Vail strolling through Vail Village and taking in the lights and beautiful sights and sounds. After a one-man celebration dinner at Sweet Basil, Vail's number-one rated restaurant, I returned to my room to pack for my flight back to the Twin Cities the next morning.

CHAPTER TWENTY-ONE

Heading Home

On Saturday morning, my shuttle pickup was at 6:00 a.m., plenty of time to get me to Eagle for the 7:58 a.m. flight. The shuttle ride west on I-70 took me through the dark mountains, which were beginning to wake up as the sun began to rise. The silhouettes of the majestic mountains were breathtaking. The harshness of mountains rising high above us, the massive, sheer presence of the rock, was truly a sight to behold. Rock hard, rock solid. Never moving in the wind, solid in both winter and summer, and beautiful from a distance or up close. These Colorado mountains helped me understand what inspiration was all about, and gave me hope for the present and future. I knew I'd miss them the moment I stepped onto the plane.

The panoramic beauty of mountains couldn't help but inspire even the most jaded of characters. For a moment, I worried whether I'd be able to apply my learnings from the week in Vail when I arrived back in Minnesota, back to my real world. *Was I just more open this week, being away from home and work, after my wipeout, being in the presence of Ed and this spectacular scenery?* I thought. *Will I sustain this inspiration when I'm back home? Was this openness to new ideas and a new way of being simply a flash in the pan, or do I really have the necessary insight and motivation to make real, lasting changes in my life?*

I guessed that was up to me.

After checking in at the airport and getting settled on the plane, I shut my eyes and thought about next steps. I focused on my breathing. In and out. Relaxing. Thinking. *What will be my way?* I thought. *What specifically must I do to sustain the progress I've made this week?*

When we were in the air, I looked in the seat pocket for something to read and found a recent copy of *Fast Company* magazine. I thumbed through the issue and noticed an article titled "Making Your Vision and Goals Real." There couldn't have been a more perfect article to read on the way home.

I couldn't believe the coincidence. But then I realized that I'd already flipped through this month's issue of the magazine, and completely blew by that article. I could hear Ed's voice in my head. "It's no coincidence, Ben. You're learning to be more self-aware. You're more present to all sorts of things, and this article is one of them. Sure, you glanced at the article before, back in Minneapolis. But this is the first time you're really *seeing* it."

I wondered what else I'd been missing by not being open to the massive amount of knowledge, advice, and support that was all around me. It was there all the time, I just hadn't been aware enough to fully experience it. I turned to the article.

The central point of the piece was that leaders have no shortage of future visions and goals for their organizations and themselves. The big problem, though, is in execution— making those visions and goals come alive. Too often, the inspiration gets lost, the vision and goals get put aside, and people become sidetracked. They lack the discipline to execute their plan, and settle instead for the status quo. *I can relate to that*, I thought.

The article outlined the technique of writing a letter to yourself, dated *after* you expect the vision or goal to come to fruition. The article suggested describing what achievement of the vision or goal would look and feel like in as much detail as possible. The idea is to get all the senses involved, so you can literally taste success. Doing this, the author wrote, creates a magnet-like effect that pulls you toward the goal. *Interesting idea,* I thought. *We'll have to try this for the team at work by collectively developing an article on what a successful year will look like. We could pick December 31 for the date. We'll assume we'll have a flawless launch of the* CyberLaser. *We'll exceed our operating plan. We'll be working great together as a team. This has possibilities,* I told myself. Then I decided to spend the rest of the flight writing my own letter that listed the positive changes I wanted to make during the year. I pulled out my note pad and began scribbling away. I visualized the end of the year, and the satisfaction I would feel if I made progress on each of these topics.

I began to write.

Dear Ben:

As this year comes to a close, it makes some sense to reflect on the past twelve months—the good and bad, the ups and downs. This year has been a breakthrough for you on many fronts. You've made excellent strides on a personal, family, and professional basis. Let's re-cap the year:

Personal

Following your February trip to Vail, you've imple-mented a solid daily routine that you've done a fine job in sticking with. Specifically, you are: exercising five times per week, thirty minutes of cardio four times a week and weightlifting three times a week; and practicing mindful-ness, a routine that includes daily breathing meditation, daily appreciation, journaling, and living on intention.

Family

You're balancing work and family much more effec-tively and doing a good overall job of being in the present with Nancy, Jeff, and Amber (with continued progress required). You're periodically using the "relationship wheel" and making adjustments where necessary to improve the health of key relationships. And you're scheduling time just to "be" with the family, including making an effort to be home for dinner at least three nights per week, you've taken a ski trip to Vail—and a family lesson with Ed! You've spent more time on the lake this summer after buying a jet ski for the family, and you've concentrated on one-on-one time with both kids and Nancy.

<u>Work</u>

At work, we beat our operating plan! We finished our year at 106 percent. We've developed a cohesive, high-performing top team, and I've improved relationships with each direct report and my boss, Mike Cole. I've made a real effort to try and get to know Mike better as a person, and our relationship has improved considerably as a result. We had fresh start discussions with each member of the team. I've discussed my development objectives and continue asking for feedforward regularly—on an ongoing basis. I hired an executive coach to keep me on track and offer other ideas to help me be my best. I'm concentrating on my personal development objectives, including focusing on using more positive leadership styles of visionary, coaching and participative; working with the team on ways to improve our working climate; improving my self-awareness by making ongoing time for reflection, meditation, and journaling; and placing an ongoing focus on "win-win" solutions.

I've also implemented monthly update meetings with Mike Cole, clarified my leadership VOICE and communicated that to my team, and implemented monthly coaching sessions with each direct report. During these sessions, we focus on what is going well, and what isn't;

talk about how they are doing with their direct reports, peers, and me; discuss their suggestions for improvement; address areas where I can be of help; and address areas where I can improve.

We implemented an executive development program for our management team to include assessments and coaching on emotional intelligence, leadership styles, and organizational climate.

Ben, you've made truly significant progress this year. Congratulations to you. While it hasn't been easy and you're still not totally "there" yet, you are on the right path. Keep up the great work!

Your best friend,

Ben

I looked over the letter. What a year this was going to be. *This will be awesome,* I thought, *if I can pull it off.* Just writing it down made it seem much more real. *If I can see, hear, smell it, and touch it,* I thought, *maybe we can make it happen.* I vowed to revisit the letter every month to keep me on track. I knew it was going to be hard work, but it was a challenge I was looking forward to. I felt my competitive juices flowing.

As we began our descent to the Minneapolis-St. Paul airport, the familiar sprawl of Lake Minnetonka came into view. It was a spectacularly sunny morning. The lake was covered with snow, but it was easy to make out the interconnected lakes and bays that unmistakably identify this large body of water as the most famous lake in the Twin Cities. At almost fifteen thousand acres, it's the tenth largest lake in Minnesota. And in a state that boasts more than ten thousand lakes, you can imagine that the tenth largest is far from a backyard pond. From twenty thousand feet or so, the lake looked as still and dead as the mountains of Colorado did. Cold and frozen, the ice was deep this time of the year—probably thirty inches or more. It was solid enough to drive trucks on. I pushed my face against the window, and spotted Gibson's Point, our street, and, for a fleeting moment, our home.

As I continued to ponder the beauty of the lake, even in the dead of winter, I began to think about the essence of the lake—water. *Water is an element, of course, just as rock is an element,* I thought. Water makes up the lake, rock makes up the mountain. The ice on the surface of the lake is solid as a rock. But unlike the mountain, underneath the ice the lake is alive, full of plants and fish. Water is truly the foundation of life. And as I thought more about water, I realized that water is an even stronger force than rock. Over time, water erodes rock, wearing it away year by year. And while you can chip away rock if you hit it with a hammer, in spite of its strength and hardness, hitting water with a hammer only gets you a rusty hammer.

I was suddenly not so worried that I would lose my learnings and motivation from Vail. I realized I discovered my source of inspiration. It was–almost literally–in my own backyard. I knew that I'd be able to reclaim this sense of anticipation and inspiration just by looking out at the lake.

As I continued to look at the beautiful body of frozen water from above and quietly reflect, I wondered something else: *Do I really need the mountains or the lake for my inspiration, after all?*

What if the inspiration simply came from—me? What if the inspiration came from within?

I read and re-read the letter I'd written myself until the plane gently touched down. The goals I'd set for myself were aggressive, yet achievable. I thought of the week I'd spent, what I'd accomplished, both on and off the mountain.

I'm going to be able to do this, I told myself, and caught a glimpse of my face in the window's reflection. Something about my expression seemed—*lighter,* somehow. Less defeated. More hopeful. The man looking back at me wasn't the same person who flew to Colorado a week ago.

I'd left the Old Ben behind in Vail.

I smiled, collected my things, and got up from my seat, joining the dozens of other passengers that had spilled into the aisle.

Welcome home, New Ben, I said to myself.

And I began to move forward.

RECOMMENDED READING

Boyatzis, Richard, Goleman, Daniel, McKee, Annie. *Primal Leadership: Realizing the Power of Emotional Intelligence.* Boston: Harvard Business School Publishing, 2002

Parent, Joseph. *Zen Golf: Mastering the Mental Game.* New York: Random House, Inc., 2002.

Goleman, Daniel. *Leadership That Gets Results.* Boston: Harvard Business Review, March-April 2000.

Goleman, Daniel. *Working With Emotional Intelligence.* New York: Bantam, 1998.

The Arbinger Institute, *Leadership and Self-Deception: Getting Out of the Box.* San Francisco: Berrett-Koehler Publishers, Inc., 2000.

Trungpa, Chogyam. *Shambhala: The Sacred Path of the Warrior.* Boston: Shambhala Publications, Inc., 1984.

Walsch, Neale-Donald. *Conversations With God.* New York. G.P. Putnam's Sons, 1995.

Zinn, Jon-Kabat. *Wherever You Go There You Are: Mindfulness Meditation In Everyday Life.* New York: Hyperion, 1994.

ABOUT THE AUTHOR

Chuck Bolton is the President of The Bolton Group LLC, an executive development firm headquartered in Minneapolis, Minnesota.

Chuck is a leading executive coach working specifically with the senior leader of the enterprise and the executive's top leadership team. He assists individual executives to become their best by assessing and developing their emotional intelligence, leadership styles, and the working climate they create for others. Chuck is the developer of Top Team Check, a proprietary assessment tool and road map for extraordinary top leadership team performance. He supports the top team in creating greater clarity, building its capabilities, and increasing its commitment to achieve extraordinary results.

Chuck is the author of *Leadership Wipeout: The Story of An Executive's Crash and Rescue* (Expert Publishing, Inc., November 2005) and *Lunches at Ike's: Keys for Gaining Extraordinary Results from The Senior Leadership Team* (to be published in the summer of 2006). He is the "podcaster" of a weekly leadership broadcast, LI9 (Leadership in 9 Minutes), and publishes Creating Executive Value, a monthly e-newsletter for senior executives.

Clients Chuck serves include: Abbott Laboratories, ACE Group, America's Blood Centers, ATS Medical, Baxter Healthcare, Boston Scientific, CarboMedics, Cobe Cardiovascular, Cochlear Americas, Deephaven Capital

Management, Deutsche Bank, ELA Medical, MedSource Technologies, Memorial Blood Centers, MGI Pharma, Mitroflow, Neurologic and Orthopedic Institute of Chicago, NeuroSource, Opus Group, Sony, Sorin Biomedica, Sorin Group, St. Jude Medical, Tanox, Think Credit Union, and Tyson Foods.

Prior to launching The Bolton Group LLC in 2000, Chuck held the position of Group Vice President, Human Resources for Boston Scientific Corporation (NYSE: BSX), a $3 billion, 13,000-employee medical technology company. Prior to Boston Scientific, he held executive roles for SCIMED Life Systems Inc, Leica, Baxter Healthcare Corporation, and American Hospital Supply Corporation.

Chuck received an MBA from Keller Graduate School of Management and a BA from Saint Mary's University in Minnesota. He has received training and certification in executive coaching, emotional intelligence, resilience, and related topics from HayGroup, Corporate Coach University, Arbinger Institute, the Alliance for Strategic Leadership, and Adaptiv Learning Systems.